CW00455115

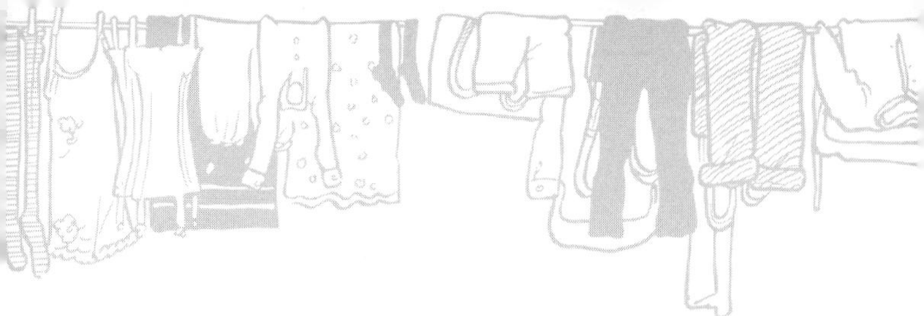

THE BROONS®

Maw Broon's Guide Tae Life

THE BROONS

Maw Broon's Guide Tae Life

BLACK & WHITE PUBLISHING

First published 2016
by Black & White Publishing Ltd
29 Ocean Drive, Edinburgh EH6 6JL

1 3 5 7 9 10 8 6 4 2   16 17 18 19

ISBN: 978 1 910230 28 2

Text by Euan Kerr and Black & White Publishing

www.thebroons.com

A CIP catalogue record for this book is available from the British Library.

Typeset by 3btype.com
Printed and bound by Pulsio SARL

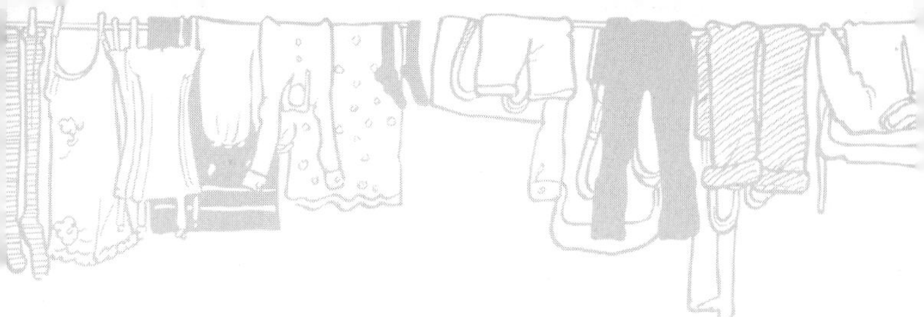

Introduction

I ken a thing or twa aboot running a household. I should do anyway. I've been the heid of The Broons family for mair years than I care tae remember! They ken wha wears the apron aroond here!

When it comes tae cooking, cleaning, home renovations, etiquette, raising children, resolving family fechts and keeping the spark alive with yer man, I've learnt a trick or twa ower the years – usually the hard way! An' ye lucky readers are goin' tae be let in on ma wee secrets!

Get stuck in tae my new book, and ye'll get tae see a' the hilarious times that ma family fell short o' ma advice and I was left black-affronted! I hope we'll gie ye a richt guid laugh as ye learn hoo tae live like a Broon!

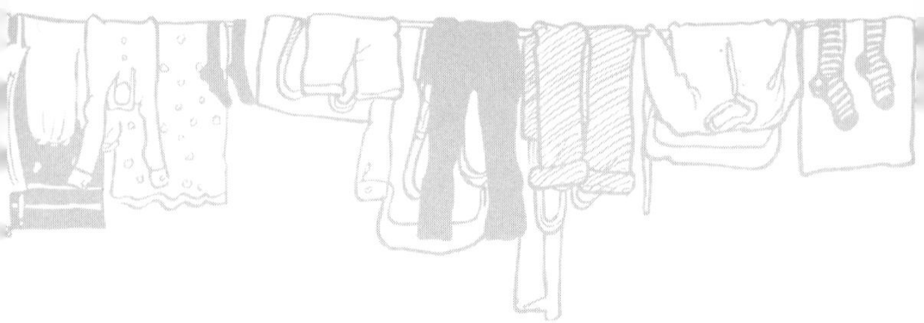

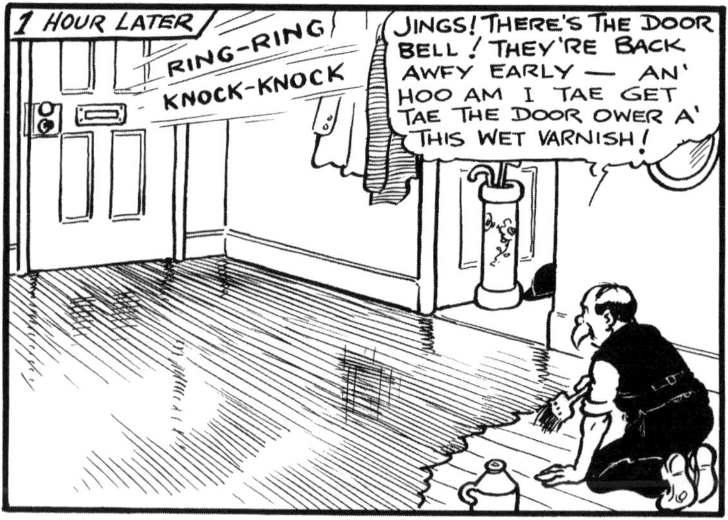
1 HOUR LATER
RING-RING
KNOCK-KNOCK
JINGS! THERE'S THE DOOR BELL! THEY'RE BACK AWFY EARLY — AN' HOO AM I TAE GET TAE THE DOOR OWER A' THIS WET VARNISH!

Planning ahead prevents
future difficulties.

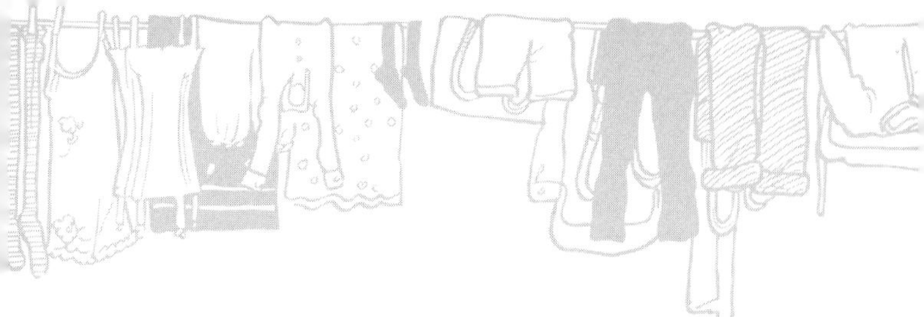

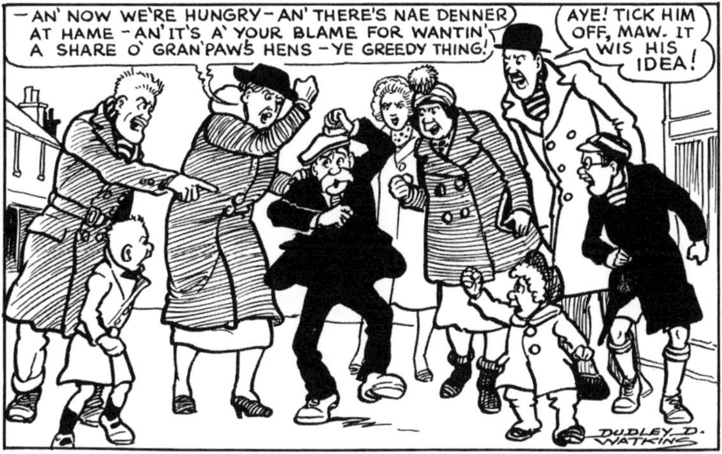

— AN' NOW WE'RE HUNGRY — AN' THERE'S NAE DENNER AT HAME — AN' IT'S A' YOUR BLAME FOR WANTIN' A SHARE O' GRAN'PAW'S HENS — YE GREEDY THING!
AYE! TICK HIM OFF, MAW. IT WIS HIS IDEA!
DUDLEY D. WATKINS

Always treat the man
of the house with the respect
that he deserves.

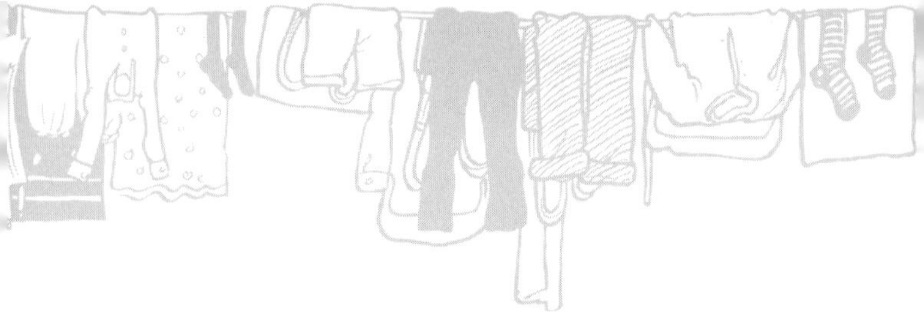

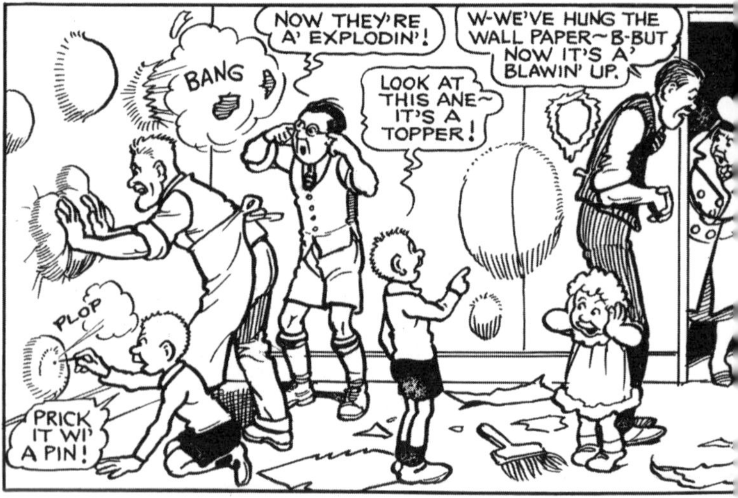

BANG
NOW THEY'RE A' EXPLODIN'!
W-WE'VE HUNG THE WALL PAPER~B-BUT NOW IT'S A' BLAWIN' UP.
LOOK AT THIS ANE~ IT'S A TOPPER!
PLOP
PRICK IT WI' A PIN!

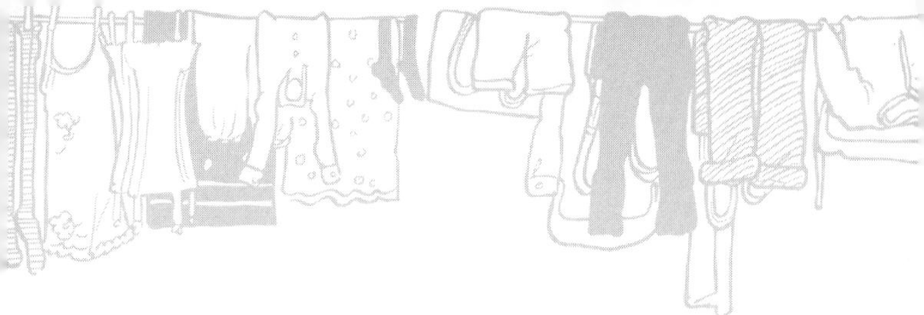

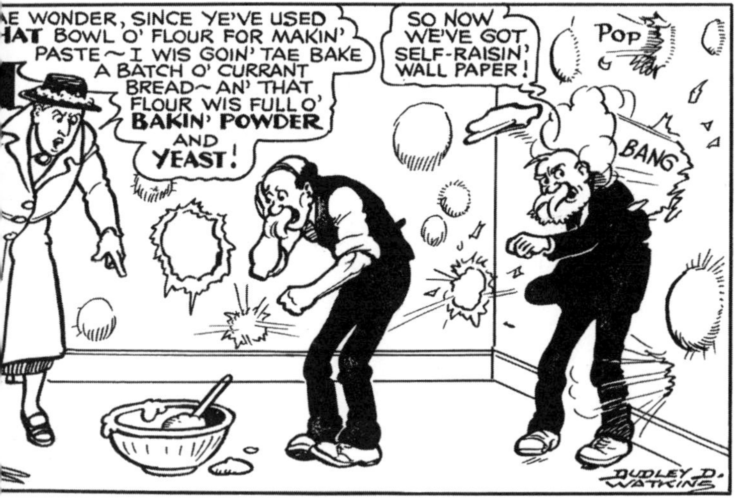
E WONDER, SINCE YE'VE USED AT BOWL O' FLOUR FOR MAKIN' PASTE ~ I WIS GOIN' TAE BAKE A BATCH O' CURRANT BREAD ~ AN' THAT FLOUR WIS FULL O' BAKIN' POWDER AND YEAST!
SO NOW WE'VE GOT SELF-RAISIN' WALL PAPER!
POP
BANG
DUDLEY D. WATKINS

Save money on expensive painters and decorators by enlisting your family's help.

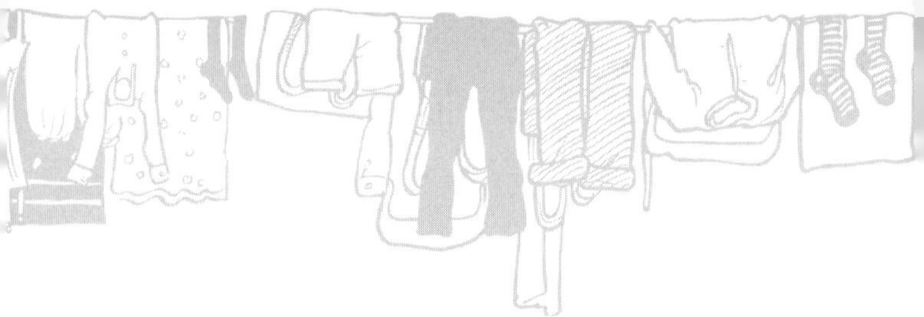

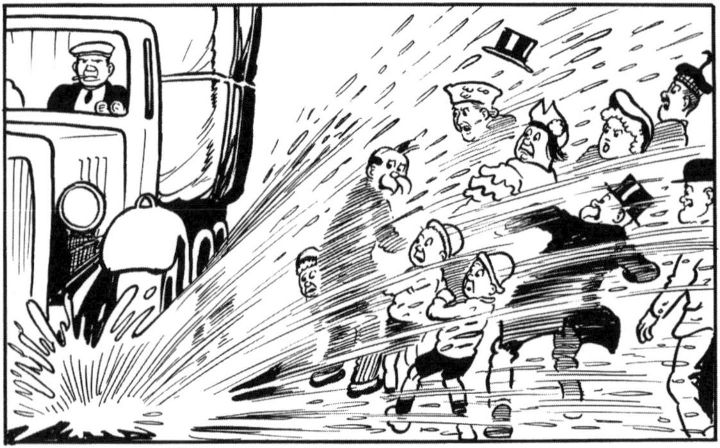

It's important to keep
your family
smartly turned out.

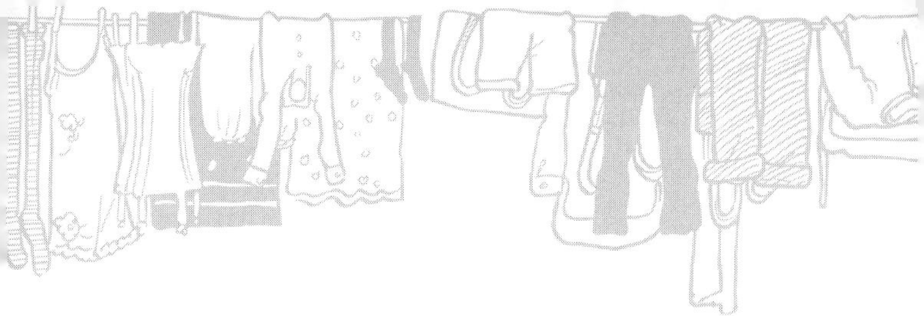

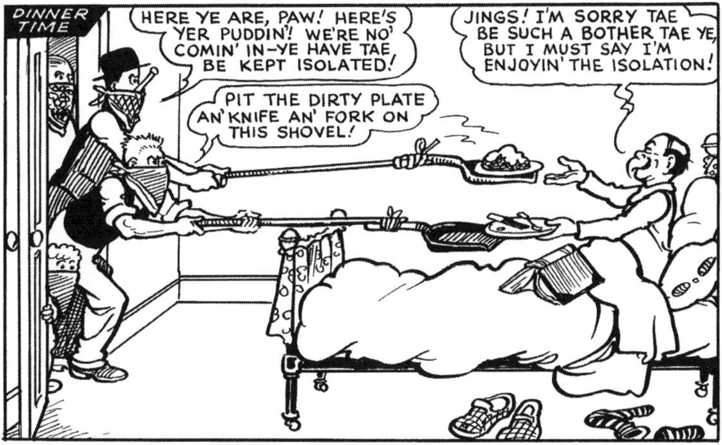

DINNER TIME
HERE YE ARE, PAW! HERE'S YER PUDDIN'! WE'RE NO' COMIN' IN—YE HAVE TAE BE KEPT ISOLATED!
PIT THE DIRTY PLATE AN' KNIFE AN' FORK ON THIS SHOVEL!
JINGS! I'M SORRY TAE BE SUCH A BOTHER TAE YE, BUT I MUST SAY I'M ENJOYIN' THE ISOLATION!

Germs can be passed easily.
Take precautions
when dealing with the sick.

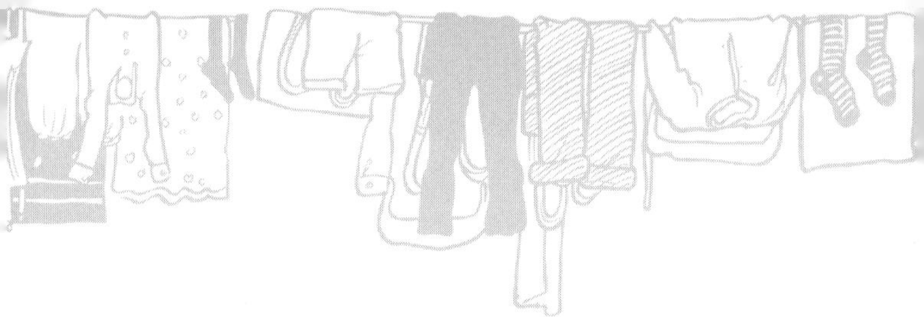

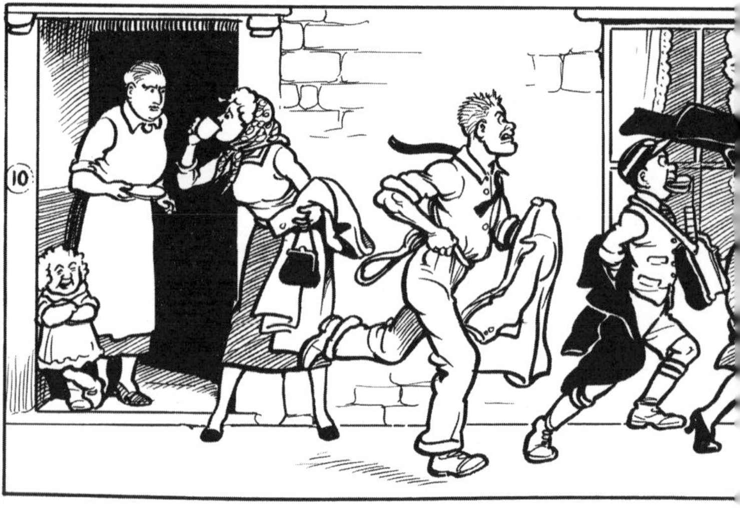
10

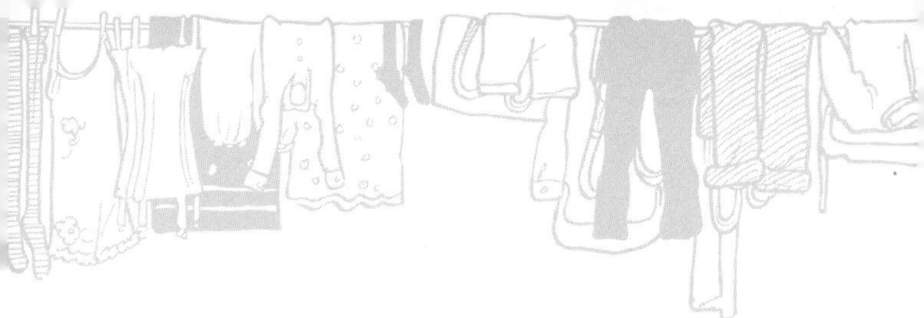

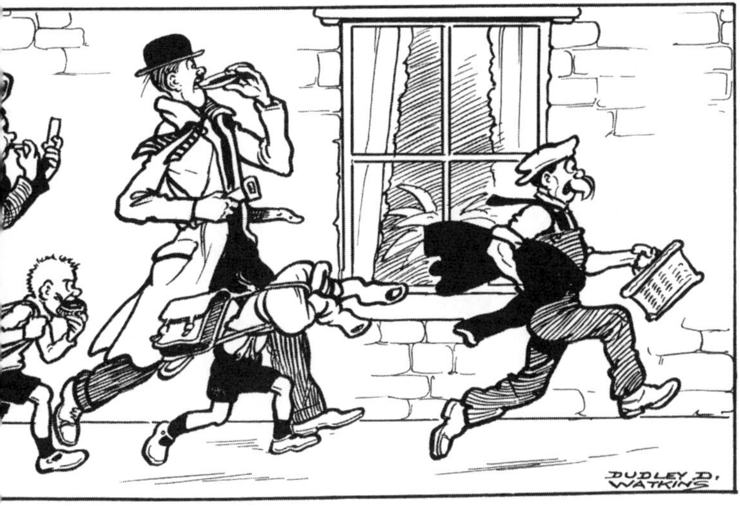
DUDLEY D. WATKINS

When getting your family ready,
always allow ample time.

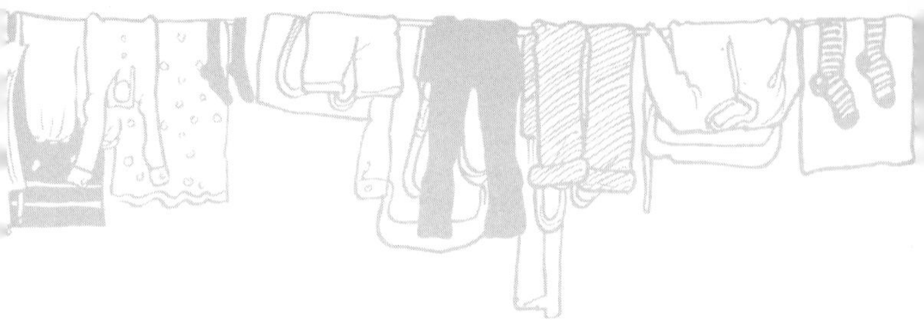

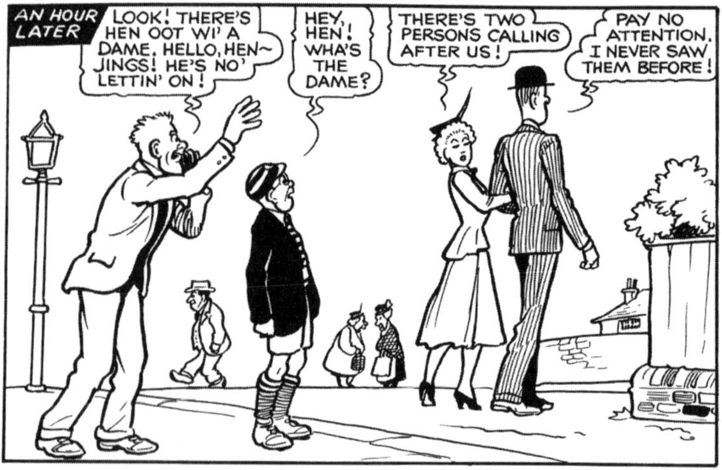
AN HOUR LATER
LOOK! THERE'S HEN OOT WI' A DAME. HELLO, HEN~ JINGS! HE'S NO' LETTIN' ON!
HEY, HEN! WHA'S THE DAME?
THERE'S TWO PERSONS CALLING AFTER US!
PAY NO ATTENTION. I NEVER SAW THEM BEFORE!

If you are the link between two people who have never met, it's up to you to make the introductions.

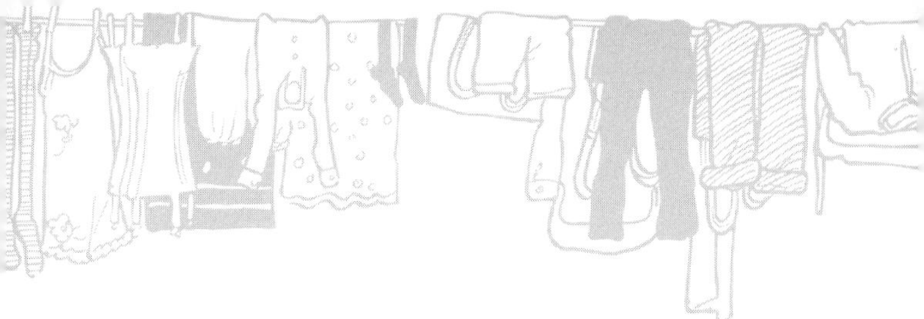

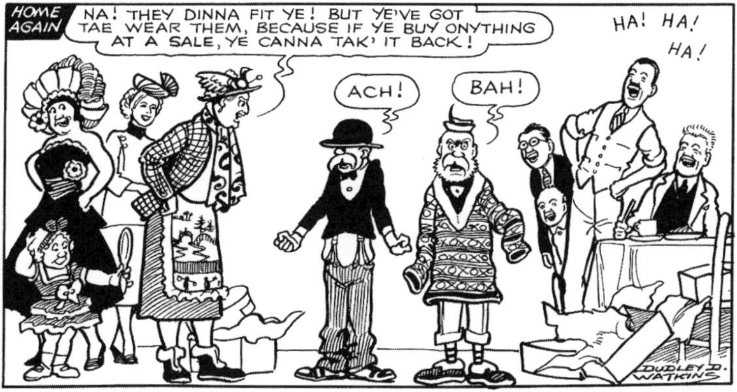
HOME AGAIN
NA! THEY DINNA FIT YE! BUT YE'VE GOT TAE WEAR THEM, BECAUSE IF YE BUY ONYTHING AT A SALE, YE CANNA TAK' IT BACK!
ACH!
BAH!
HA! HA! HA!
DUDLEY D. WATKINS

Always check the small print
when buying items on sale.

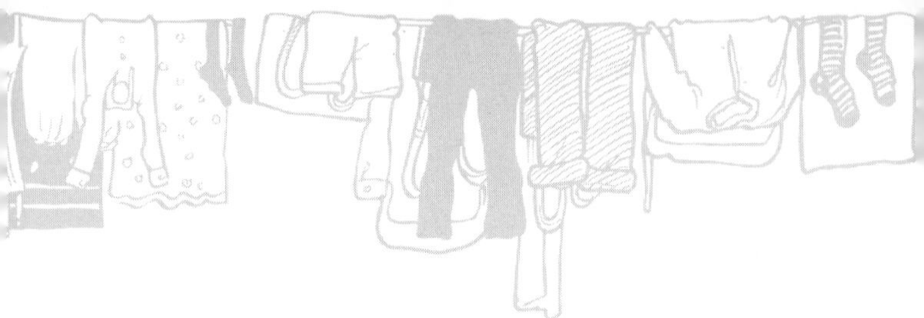

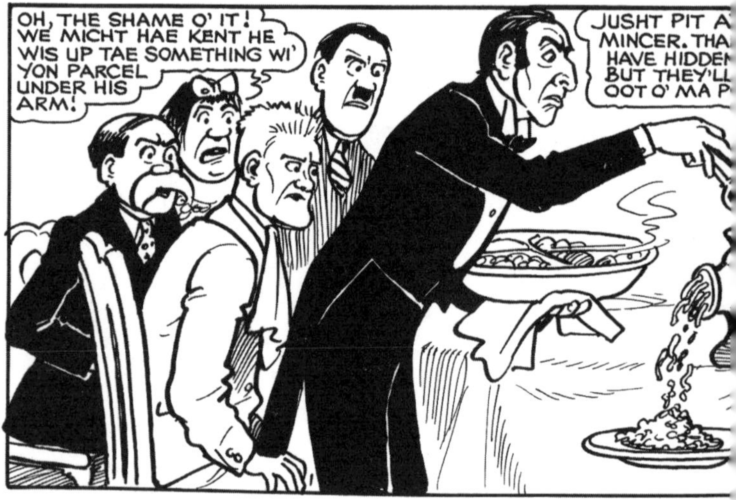
OH, THE SHAME O' IT! WE MICHT HAE KENT HE WIS UP TAE SOMETHING WI' YON PARCEL UNDER HIS ARM!
JUSHT PIT A MINCER. THA HAVE HIDDE BUT THEY'LL OOT O' MA P

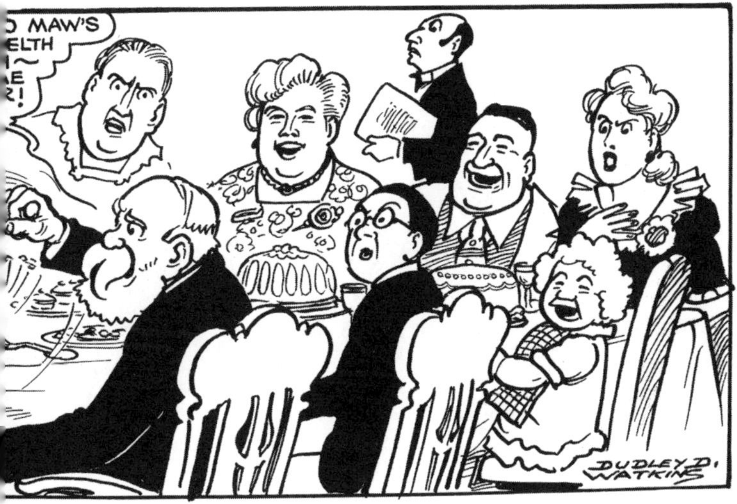
MAW'S
DUDLEY D. WATKINS

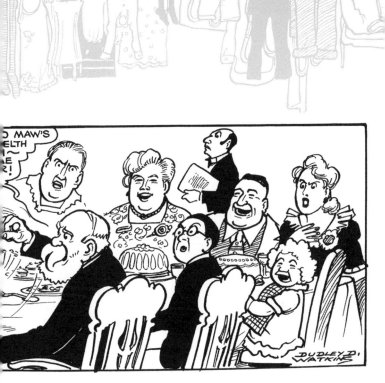

When it comes to dining out, do not be afraid to make special requests.

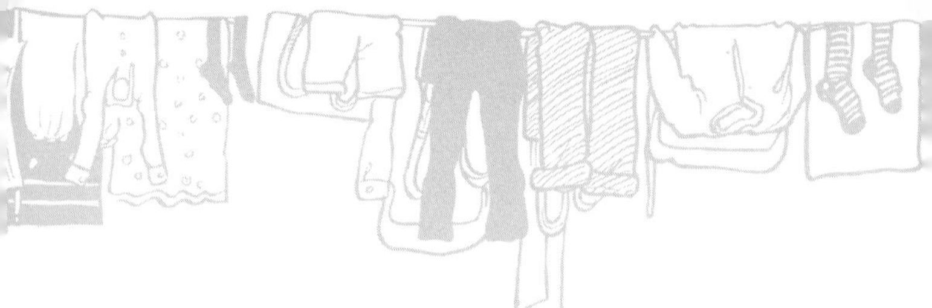

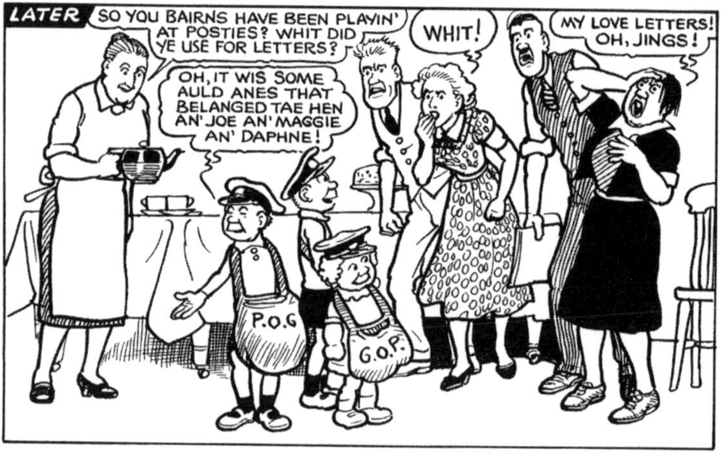
LATER
SO YOU BAIRNS HAVE BEEN PLAYIN' AT POSTIES? WHIT DID YE USE FOR LETTERS?
OH, IT WIS SOME AULD ANES THAT BELANGED TAE HEN AN' JOE AN' MAGGIE AN' DAPHNE!
WHIT!
MY LOVE LETTERS! OH, JINGS!
P.O.G
G.O.P.

Encourage your children
to develop their imagination.

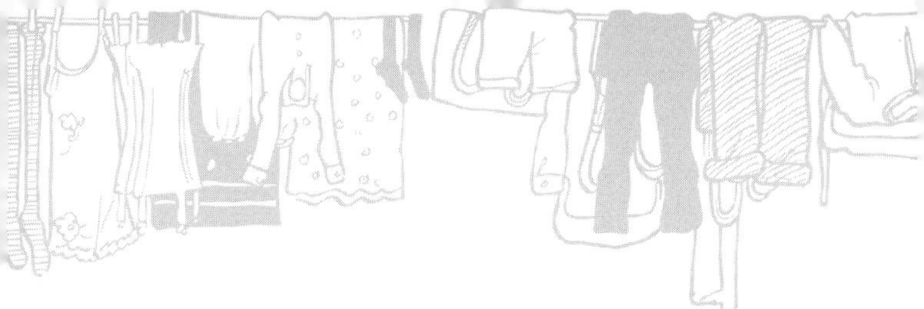

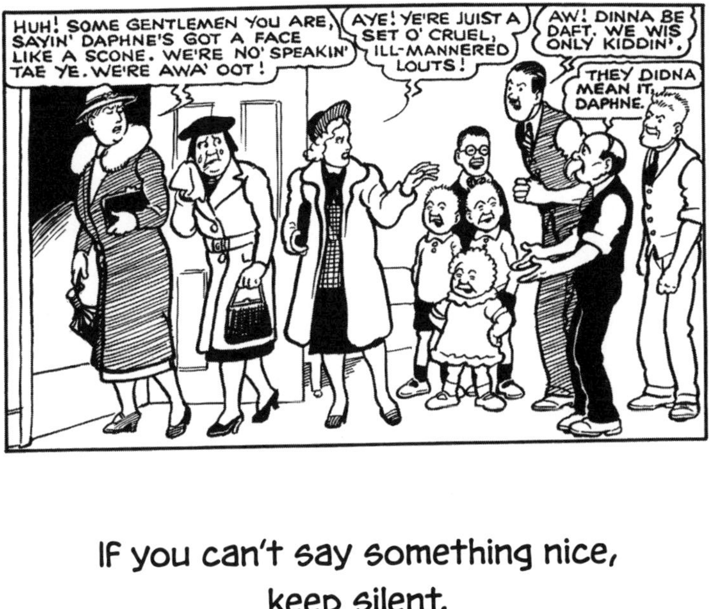

HUH! SOME GENTLEMEN YOU ARE, SAYIN' DAPHNE'S GOT A FACE LIKE A SCONE. WE'RE NO' SPEAKIN' TAE YE. WE'RE AWA' OOT!
AYE! YE'RE JUIST A SET O' CRUEL, ILL-MANNERED LOUTS!
AW! DINNA BE DAFT. WE WIS ONLY KIDDIN'.
THEY DIDNA MEAN IT, DAPHNE.

If you can't say something nice,
keep silent.

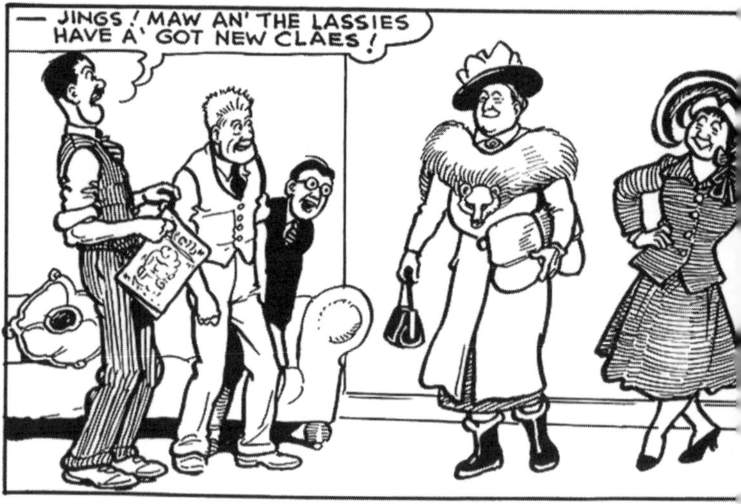
— JINGS! MAW AN' THE LASSIES HAVE A' GOT NEW CLAES!

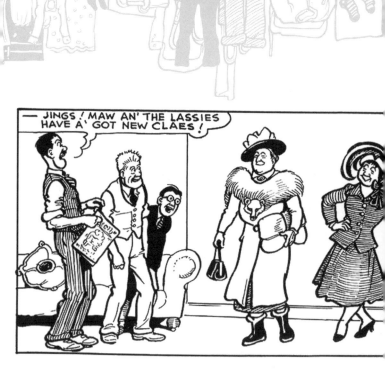

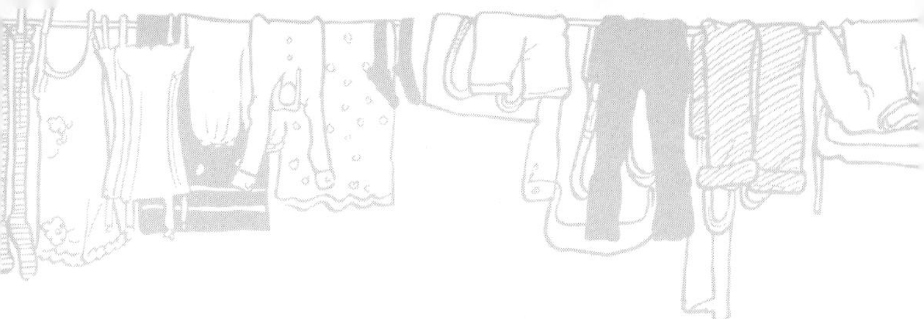

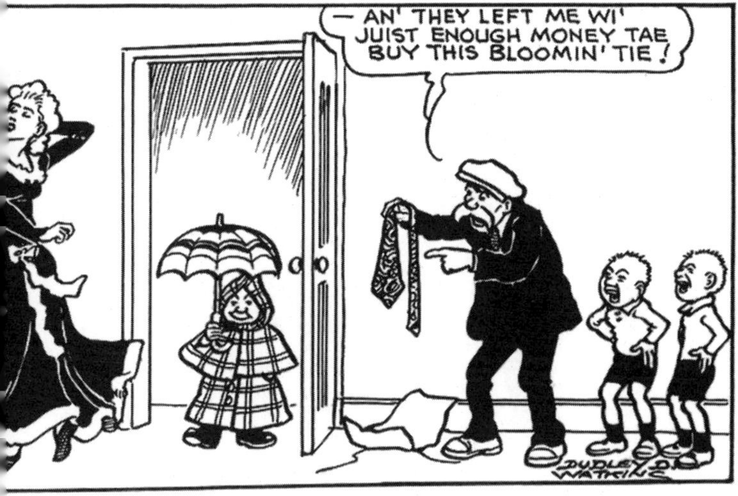
— AN' THEY LEFT ME WI' JUIST ENOUGH MONEY TAE BUY THIS BLOOMIN' TIE !
DUDLEY D. WATKINS

Ladies, always dress
in the height of fashion.

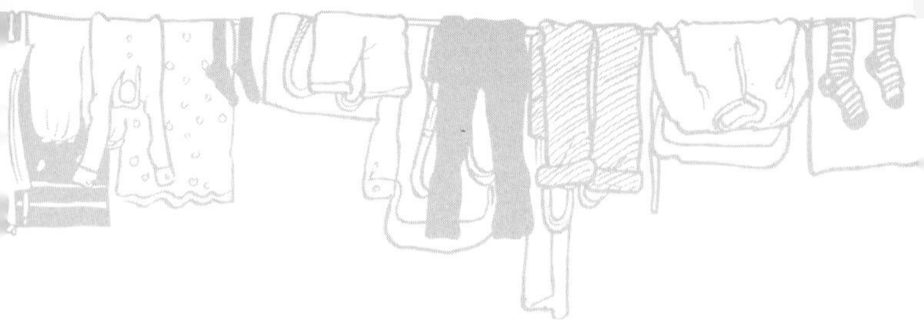

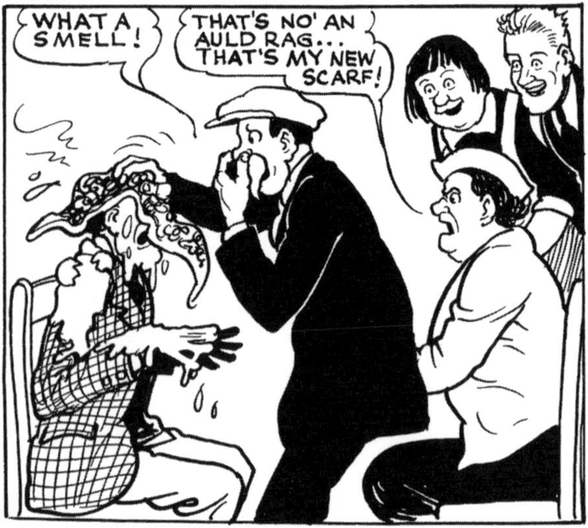
WHAT A SMELL!
THAT'S NO' AN AULD RAG... THAT'S MY NEW SCARF!

Try to make your guests feel welcome.

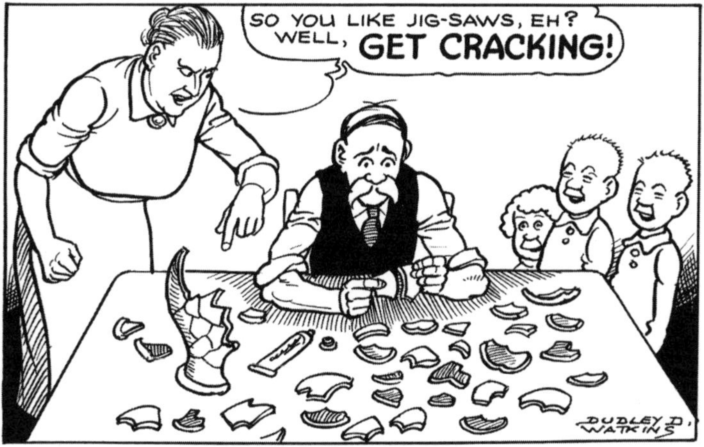
SO YOU LIKE JIG-SAWS, EH? WELL, GET CRACKING!
DUDLEY D. WATKINS

Encourage your husband
to pursue his hobbies.

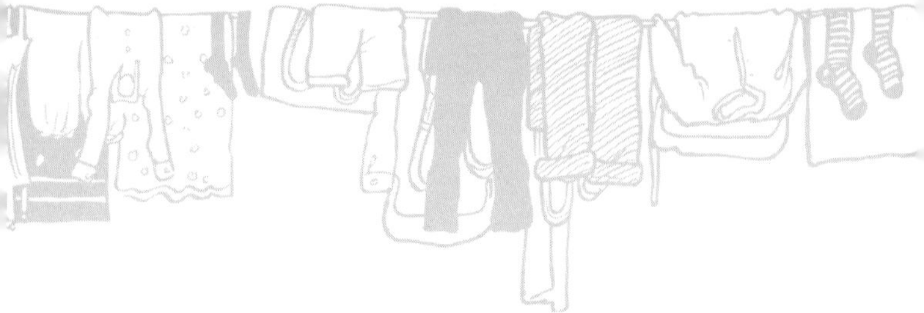

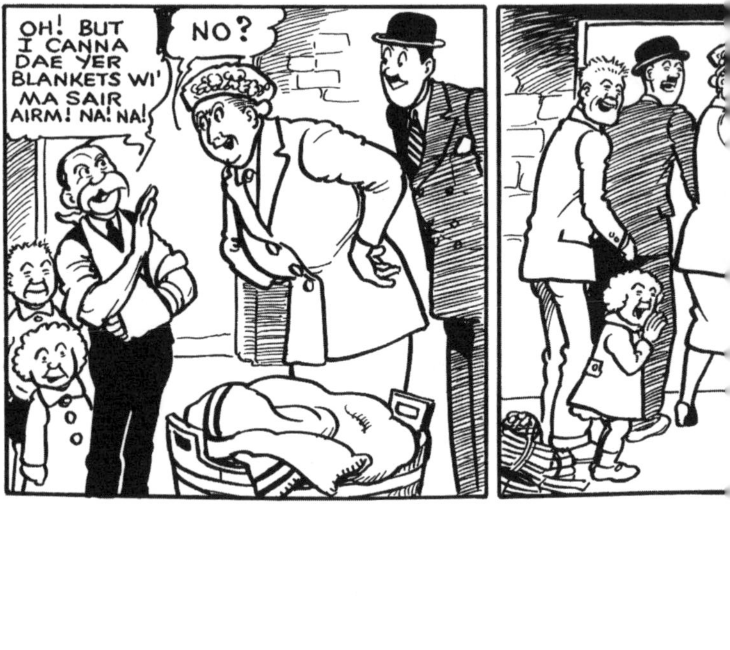
OH! BUT I CANNA DAE YER BLANKETS WI' MA SAIR AIRM! NA! NA!
NO?

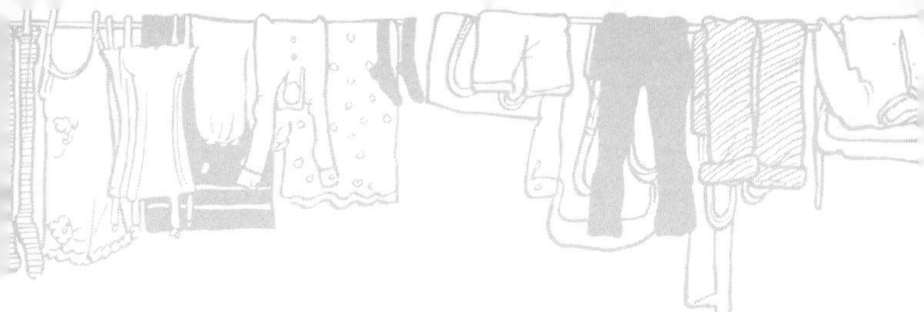

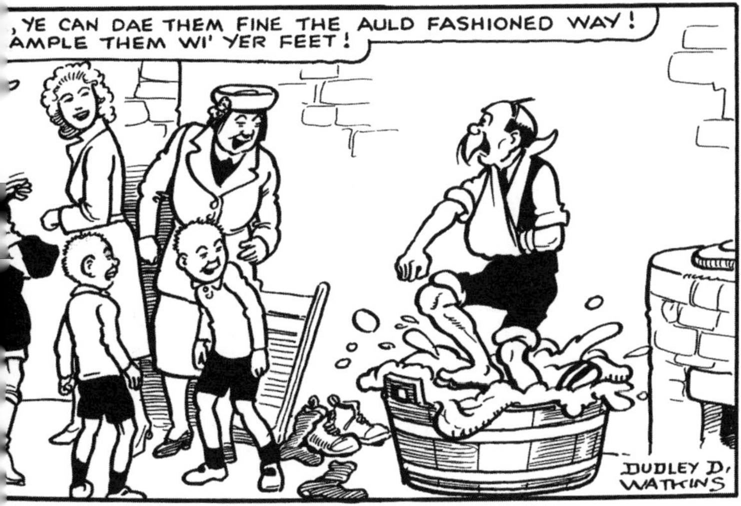
, YE CAN DAE THEM FINE THE AULD FASHIONED WAY! AMPLE THEM WI' YER FEET!
DUDLEY D. WATKINS

Sometimes the old ways are the best.

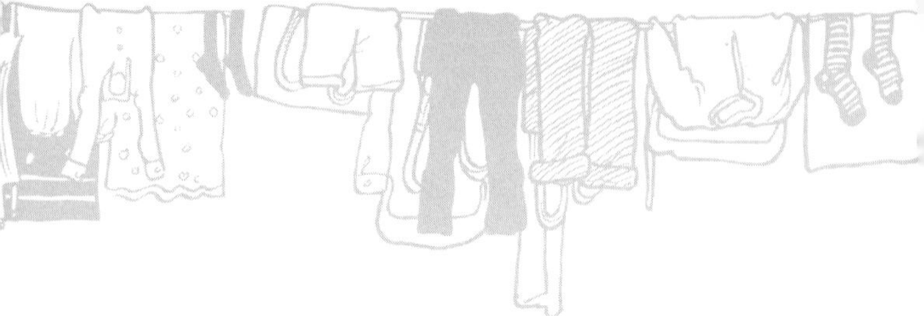

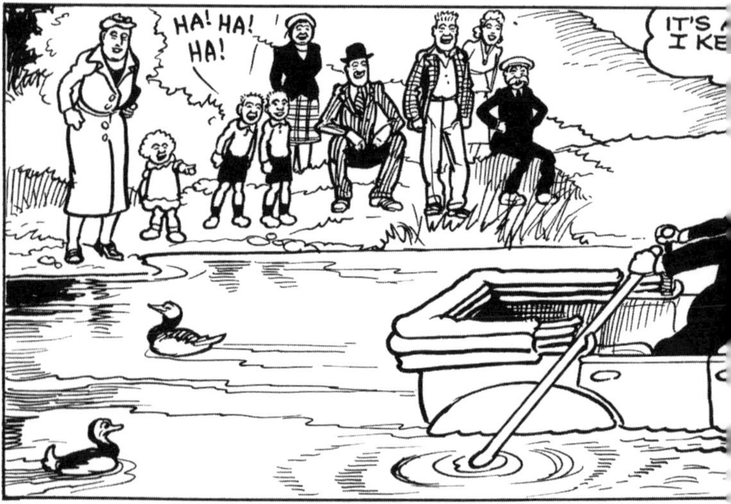
HA! HA! HA!
IT'S
I

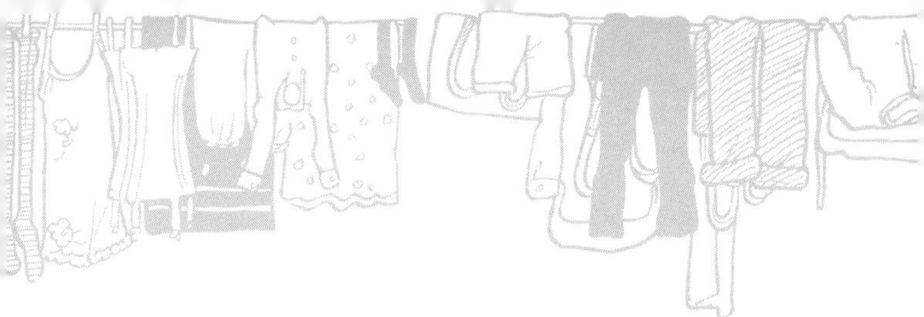

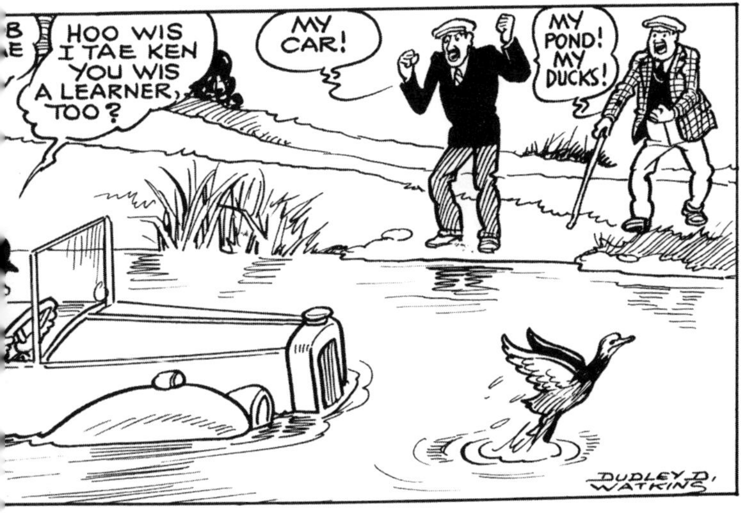
HOO WIS I TAE KEN YOU WIS A LEARNER, TOO?
MY CAR!
MY POND! MY DUCKS!
DUDLEY D. WATKINS

Learn to adapt when you find yourself in a sticky situation.

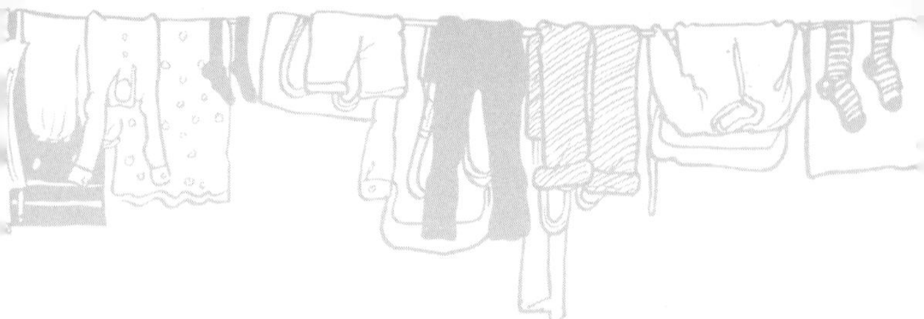

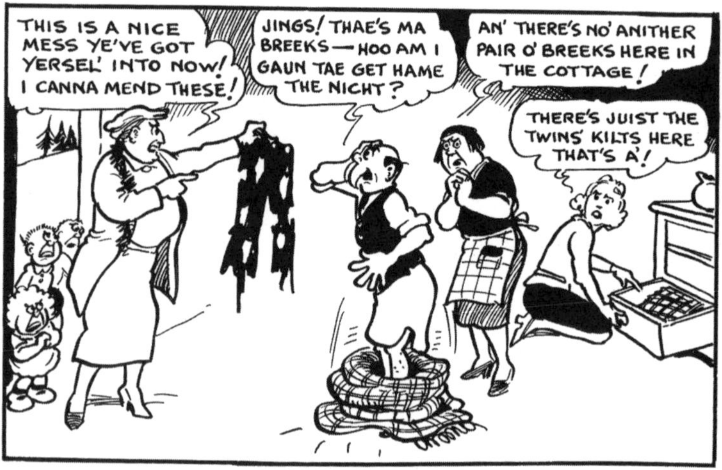
THIS IS A NICE MESS YE'VE GOT YERSEL' INTO NOW! I CANNA MEND THESE!
JINGS! THAE'S MA BREEKS—HOO AM I GAUN TAE GET HAME THE NICHT?
AN' THERE'S NO' ANITHER PAIR O' BREEKS HERE IN THE COTTAGE!
THERE'S JUIST THE TWINS' KILTS HERE THAT'S A'!

There are times when you have to admit that clothing is beyond repair.

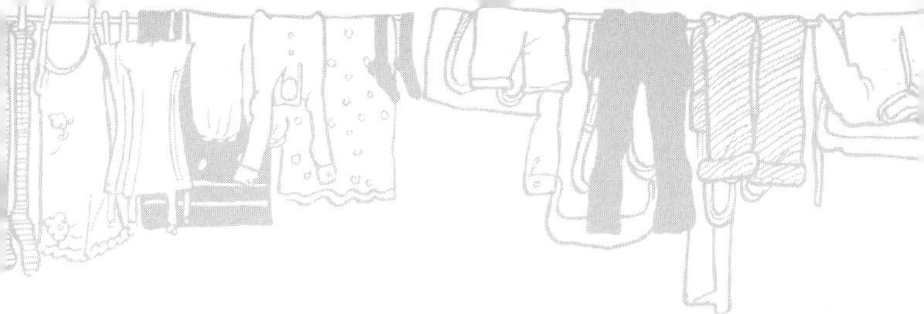

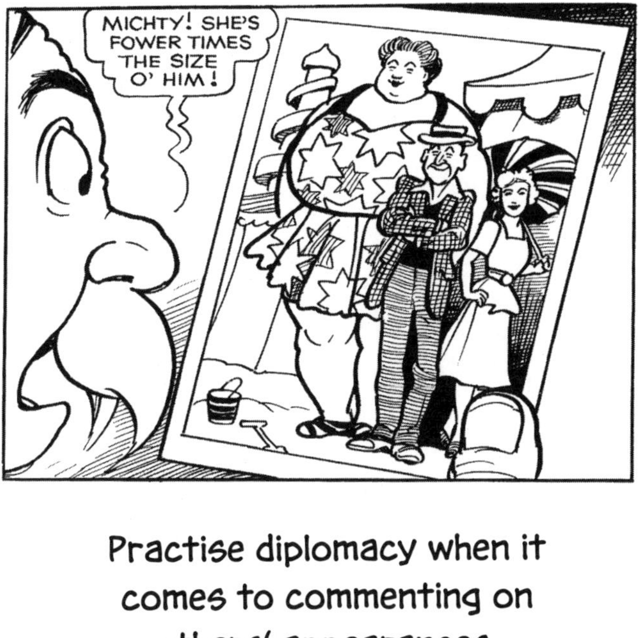
MICHTY! SHE'S FOWER TIMES THE SIZE O' HIM!

Practise diplomacy when it comes to commenting on others' appearances.

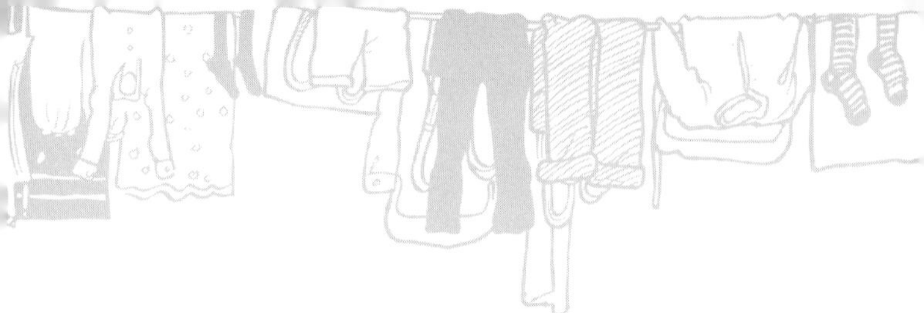

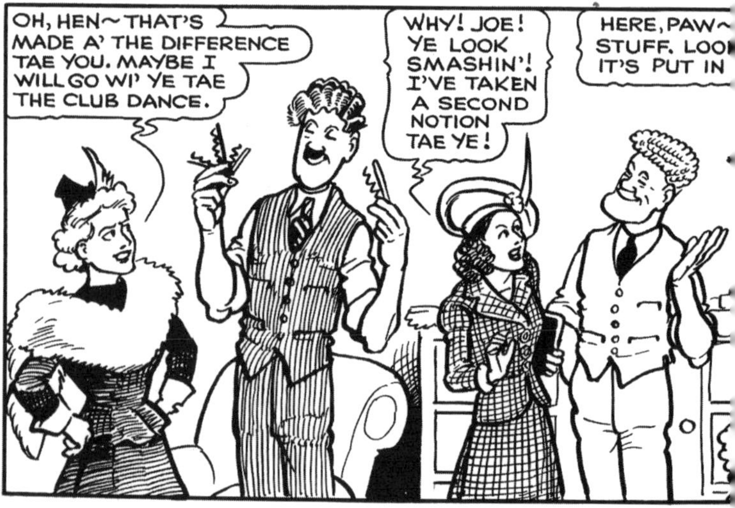

OH, HEN~THAT'S MADE A' THE DIFFERENCE TAE YOU. MAYBE I WILL GO WI' YE TAE THE CLUB DANCE.
WHY! JOE! YE LOOK SMASHIN'! I'VE TAKEN A SECOND NOTION TAE YE!
HERE, PAW~ STUFF. IT'S PUT IN

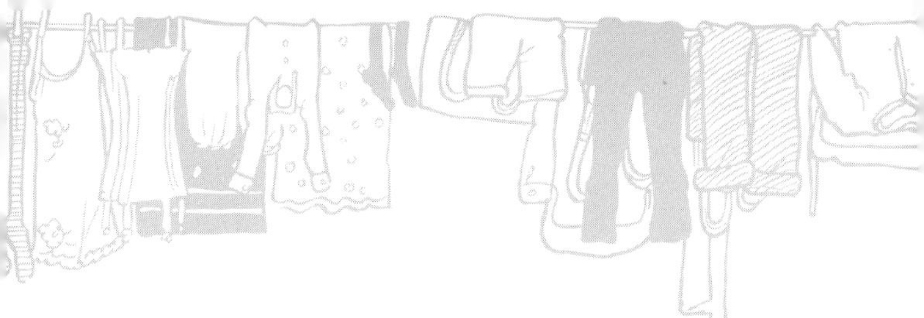

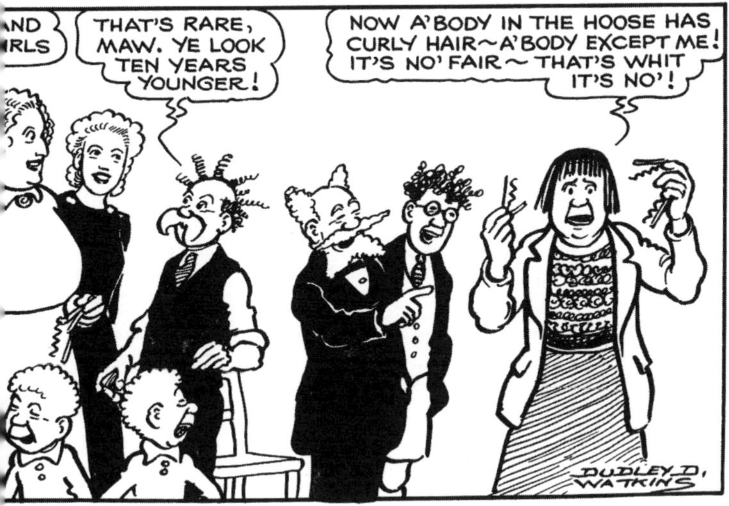
THAT'S RARE, MAW. YE LOOK TEN YEARS YOUNGER!
NOW A'BODY IN THE HOOSE HAS CURLY HAIR~A'BODY EXCEPT ME! IT'S NO' FAIR~THAT'S WHIT IT'S NO'!
DUDLEY D, WATKINS

A new hairstyle goes a long way
to keeping the spark alive.

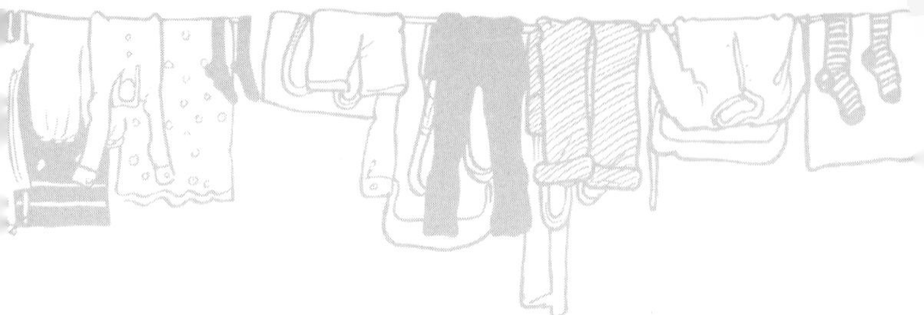

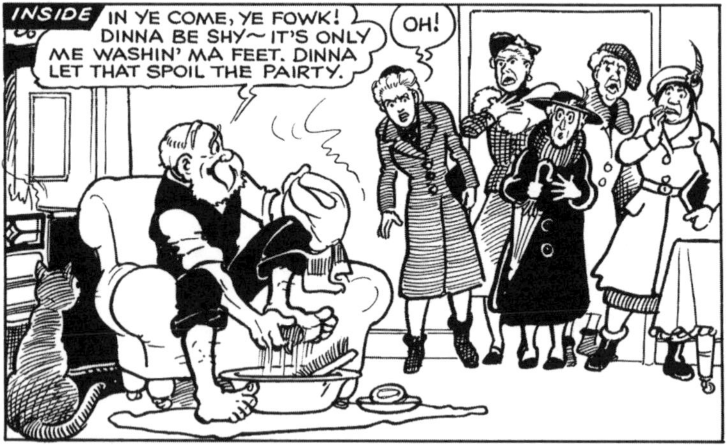
INSIDE
IN YE COME, YE FOWK! DINNA BE SHY~ IT'S ONLY ME WASHIN' MA FEET. DINNA LET THAT SPOIL THE PAIRTY.
OH!

Always perform
your ablutions in private.

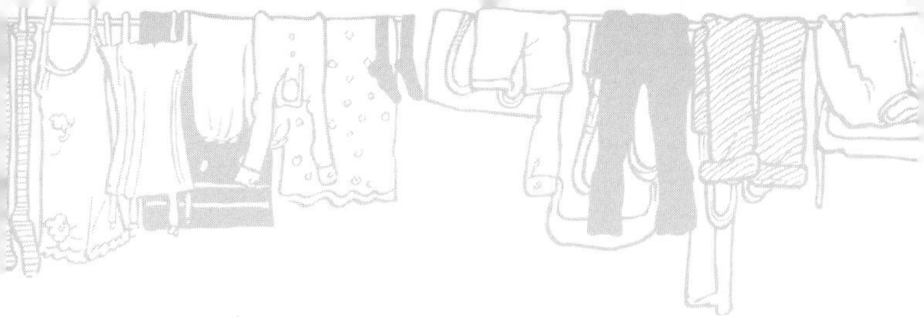

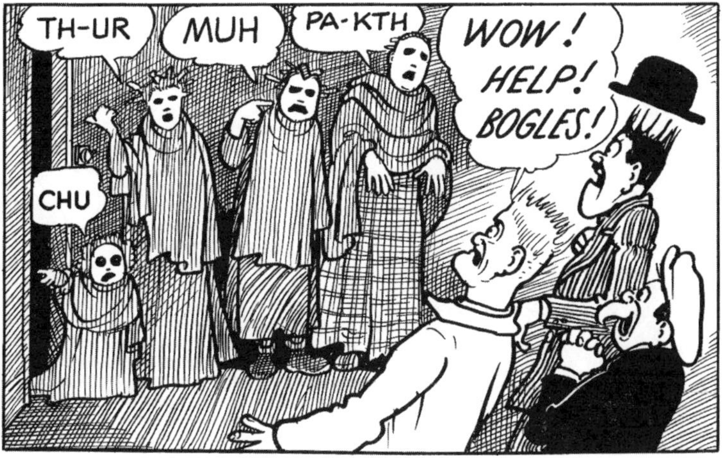

TH-UR
MUH
PA-KTH
WOW! HELP! BOGLES!
CHU

A night mask is excellent for maintaining your youthful complexion.

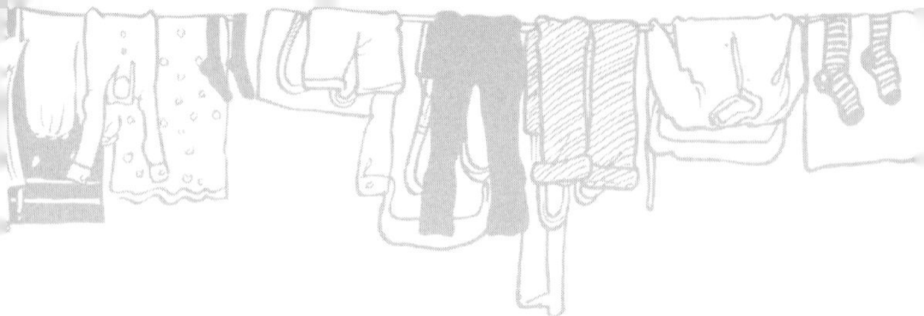

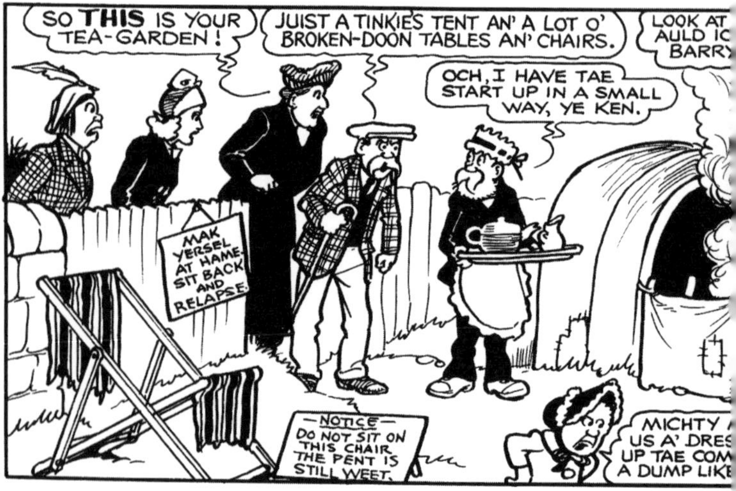

SO THIS IS YOUR TEA-GARDEN!
JUIST A TINKIE'S TENT AN' A LOT O' BROKEN-DOON TABLES AN' CHAIRS.
LOOK AT AULD IC BARR
OCH, I HAVE TAE START UP IN A SMALL WAY, YE KEN.
MAK YERSEL AT HAME. SIT BACK AND RELAPSE.
—NOTICE— DO NOT SIT ON THIS CHAIR THE PENT IS STILL WEET.
MICHTY US A' DRES UP TAE COM A DUMP LIK

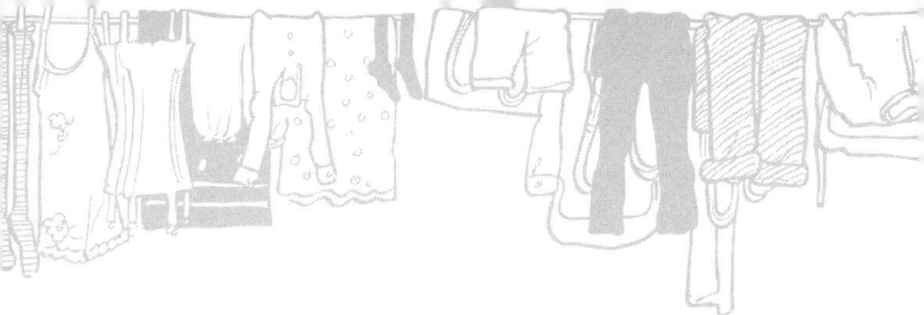

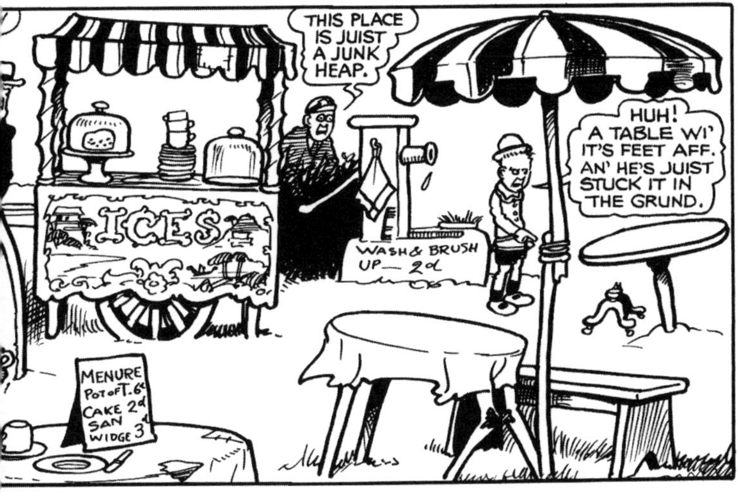
THIS PLACE IS JUIST A JUNK HEAP.
HUH! A TABLE WI' IT'S FEET AFF. AN' HE'S JUIST STUCK IT IN THE GRUND.
ICES
WASH & BRUSH UP— 2d
MENURE
POT OF T. 6d
CAKE 2d
SAN WIDGE 3d

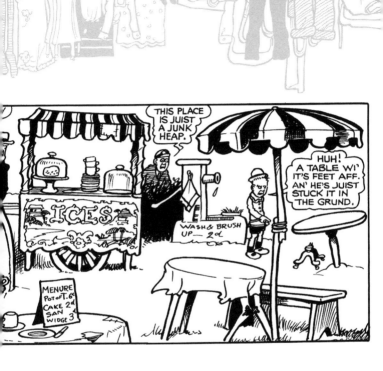

Always dress for the occasion.

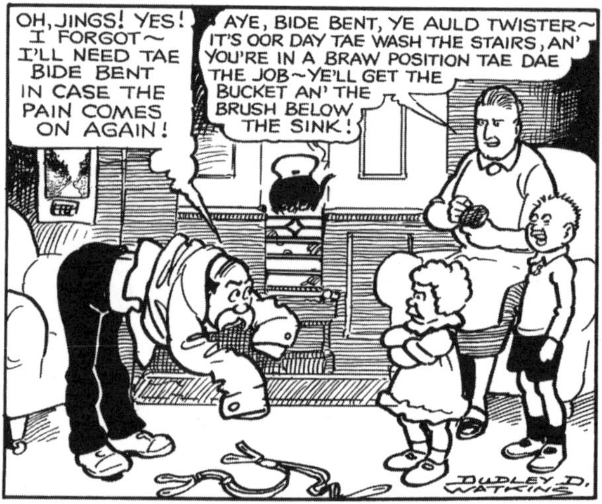
OH, JINGS! YES! I FORGOT~ I'LL NEED TAE BIDE BENT IN CASE THE PAIN COMES ON AGAIN!
AYE, BIDE BENT, YE AULD TWISTER~ IT'S OOR DAY TAE WASH THE STAIRS, AN' YOU'RE IN A BRAW POSITION TAE DAE THE JOB~YE'LL GET THE BUCKET AN' THE BRUSH BELOW THE SINK!
DUDLEY D. WATKINS

When things go wrong,
try to use the circumstances
to your advantage.

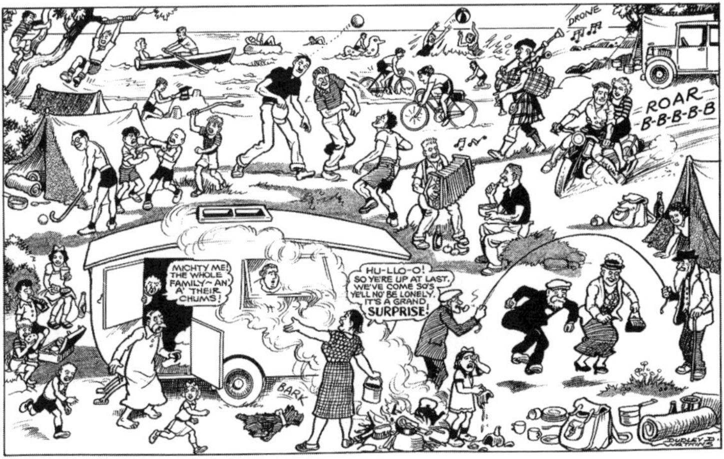
DRONE
ROAR-B-B-B-B-B
MIGHTY ME! THE WHOLE FAMILY~AN' A' THEIR CHUMS!
HU-LLO-O! SO YE'RE UP AT LAST. WE'VE COME SO'S YE'LL NO' BE LONELY. IT'S A GRAND SURPRISE!
BARK
DUDLEY D. WATKINS

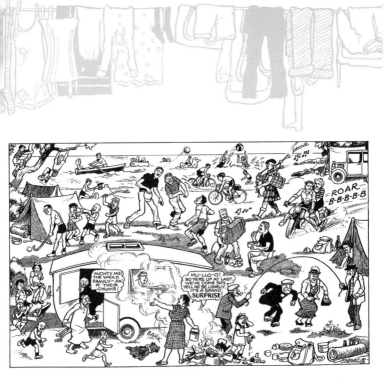

Get away from it all
in the peaceful countryside.

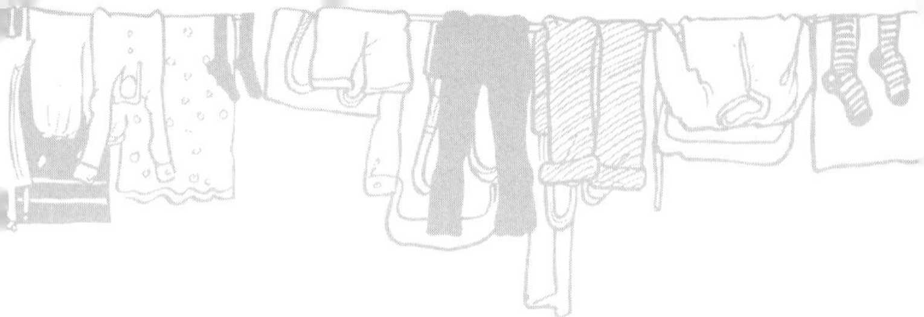

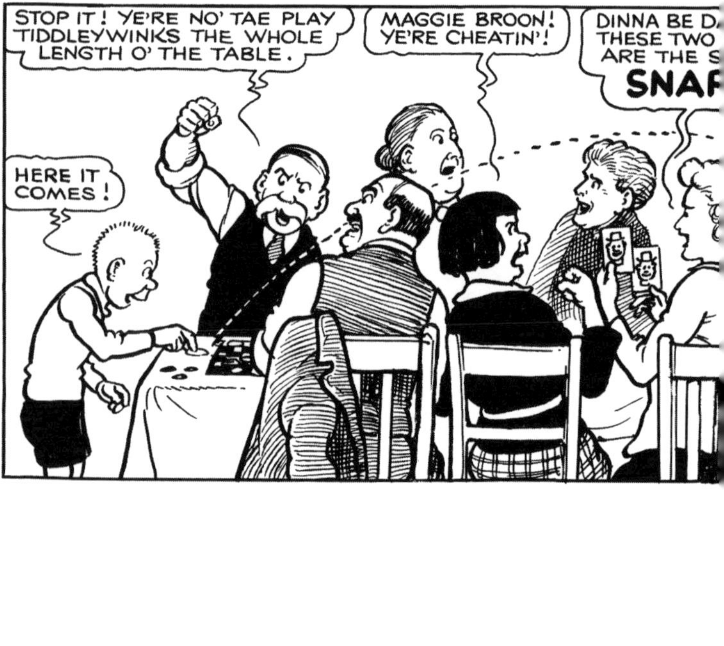
STOP IT! YE'RE NO' TAE PLAY TIDDLEYWINKS THE WHOLE LENGTH O' THE TABLE.
MAGGIE BROON! YE'RE CHEATIN'!
DINNA BE D
THESE TWO
ARE THE S
SNA
HERE IT COMES!

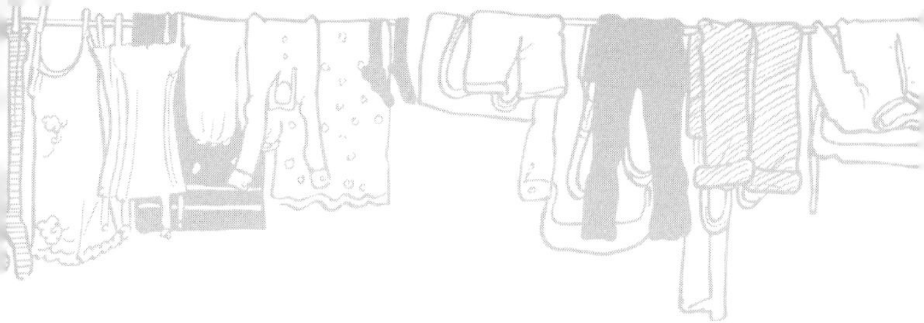

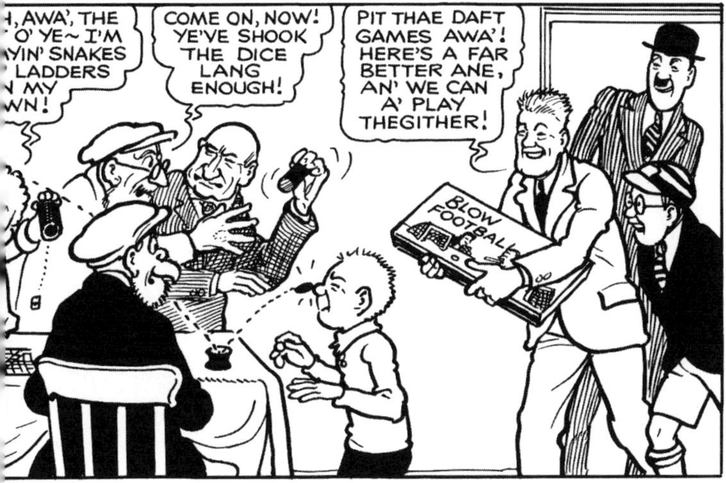
H, AWA', THE
O' YE~ I'M
YIN' SNAKES
LADDERS
N MY
WN!
COME ON, NOW! YE'VE SHOOK THE DICE LANG ENOUGH!
PIT THAE DAFT GAMES AWA'! HERE'S A FAR BETTER ANE, AN' WE CAN A' PLAY THEGITHER!
BLOW FOOTBALL

Board games are an excellent choice for peaceful family time.

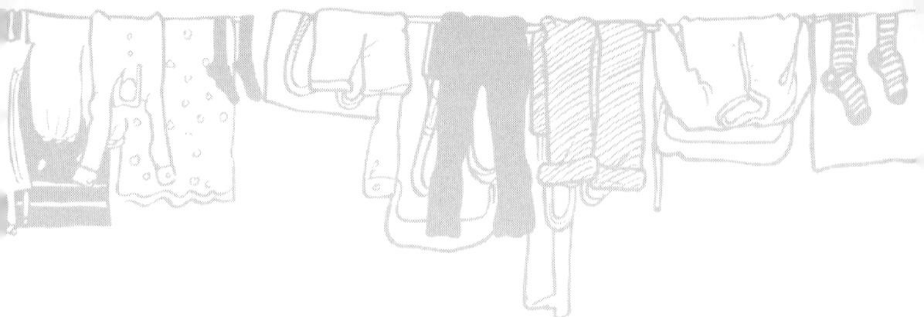

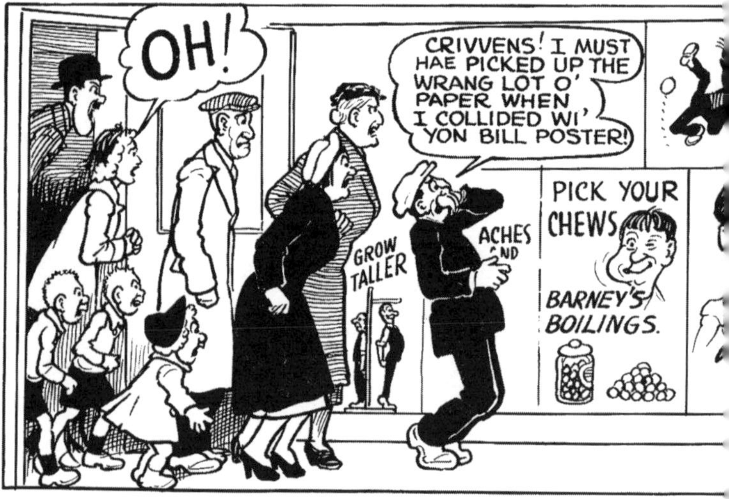
OH!
CRIVVENS! I MUST HAE PICKED UP THE WRANG LOT O' PAPER WHEN I COLLIDED WI' YON BILL POSTER!
GROW TALLER
ACHES
PICK YOUR CHEWS
BARNEY'S BOILINGS.

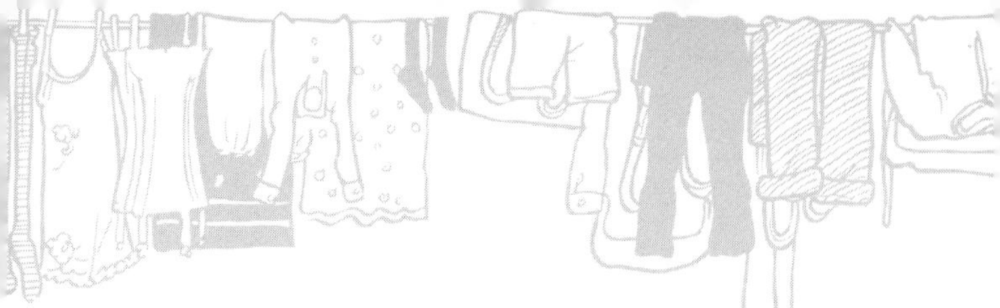

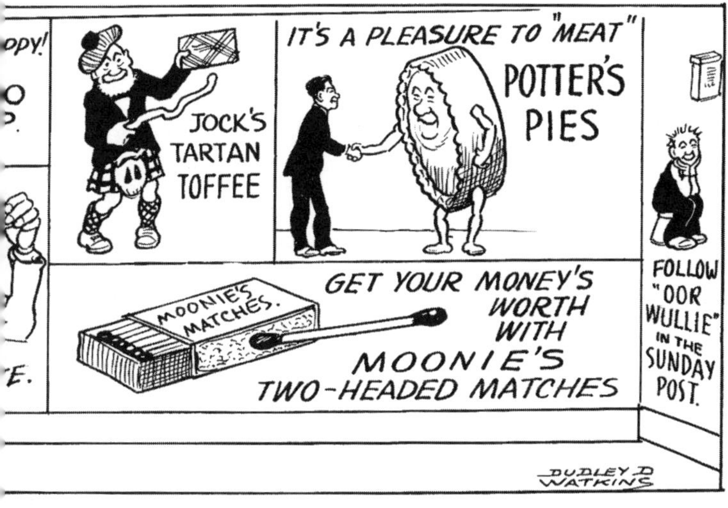

JOCK'S TARTAN TOFFEE
IT'S A PLEASURE TO "MEAT"
POTTER'S PIES
MOONIE'S MATCHES.
GET YOUR MONEY'S WORTH WITH MOONIE'S TWO-HEADED MATCHES
FOLLOW "OOR WULLIE" IN THE SUNDAY POST.
DUDLEY D WATKINS

Avoid bold choices in interior design.

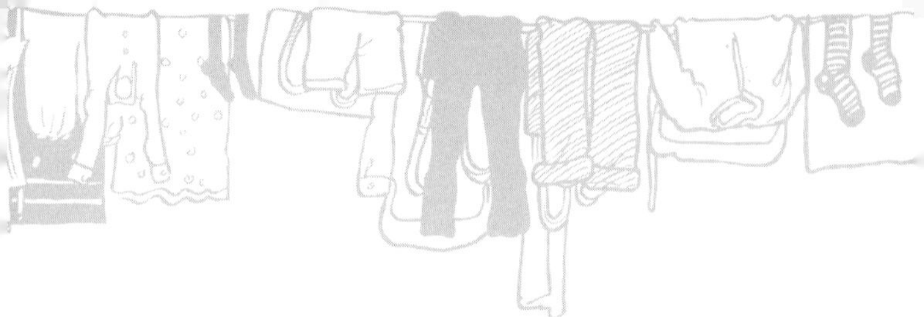

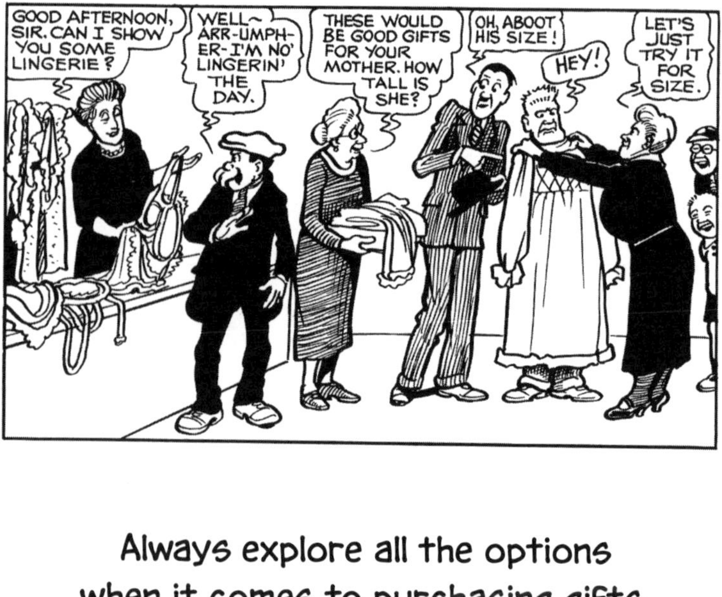
GOOD AFTERNOON, SIR. CAN I SHOW YOU SOME LINGERIE ?
WELL~ ARR-UMPH- ER-I'M NO' LINGERIN' THE DAY.
THESE WOULD BE GOOD GIFTS FOR YOUR MOTHER. HOW TALL IS SHE?
OH, ABOOT HIS SIZE!
HEY!
LET'S JUST TRY IT FOR SIZE.

Always explore all the options when it comes to purchasing gifts.

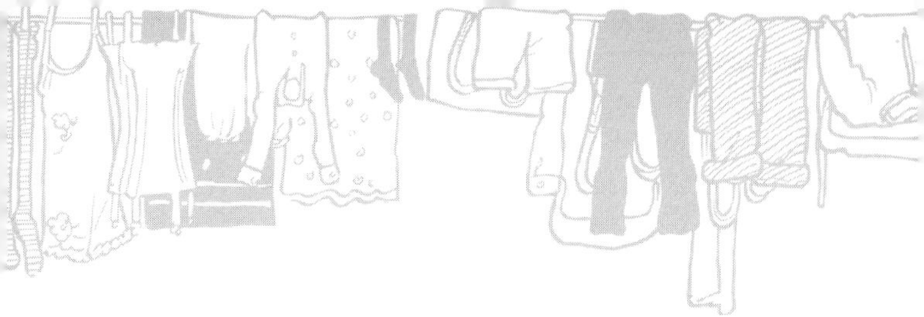

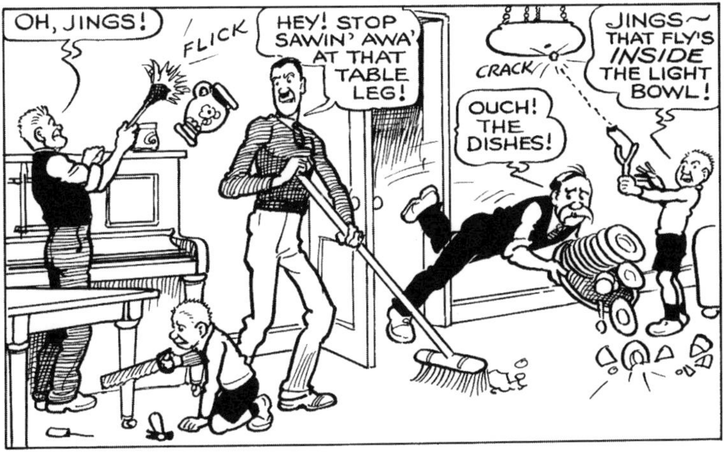

OH, JINGS!
FLICK
HEY! STOP SAWIN' AWA' AT THAT TABLE LEG!
CRACK
OUCH! THE DISHES!
JINGS~ THAT FLY'S *INSIDE* THE LIGHT BOWL!

The men of the house can offer invaluable help around the home.

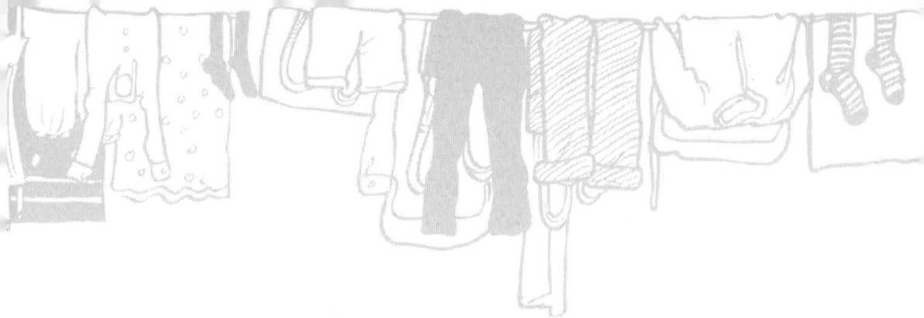

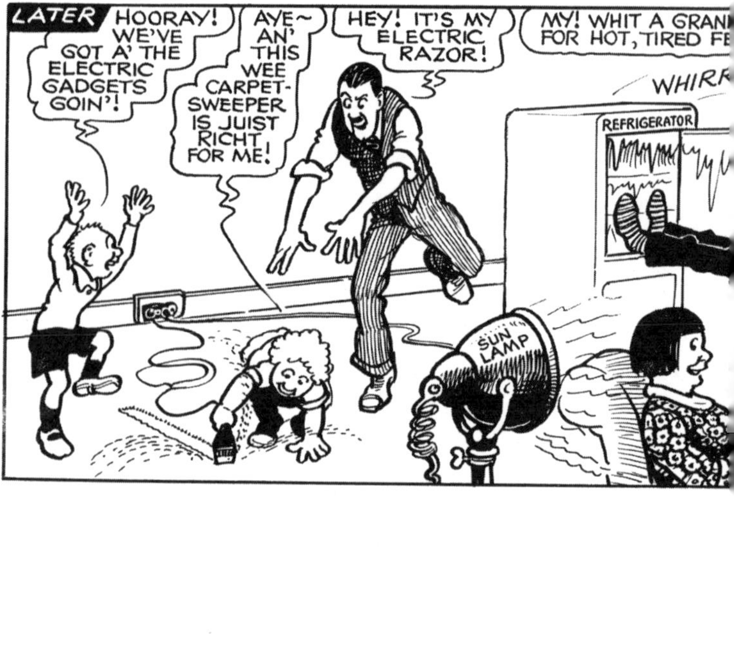
LATER
HOORAY! WE'VE GOT A' THE ELECTRIC GADGETS GOIN'!
AYE~ AN' THIS WEE CARPET-SWEEPER IS JUIST RICHT FOR ME!
HEY! IT'S MY ELECTRIC RAZOR!
MY! WHIT A GRAN
FOR HOT, TIRED FE
WHIR
REFRIGERATOR
SUN LAMP

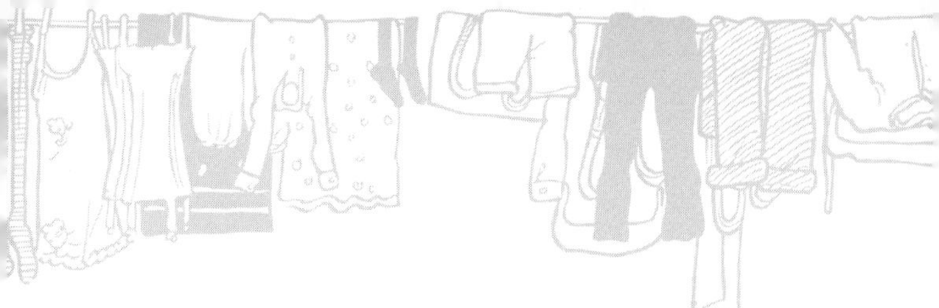

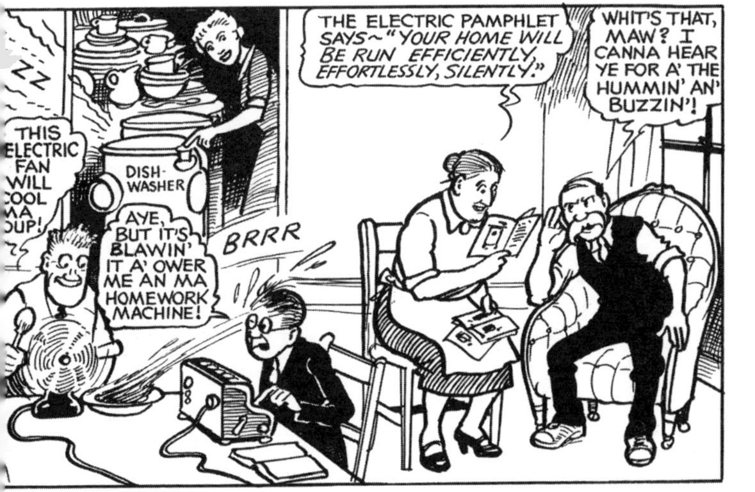

THIS ELECTRIC FAN WILL COOL MA OUP!
DISH-WASHER
AYE, BUT IT'S BLAWIN' IT A' OWER ME AN MA HOMEWORK MACHINE!
BRRR
THE ELECTRIC PAMPHLET SAYS~"YOUR HOME WILL BE RUN EFFICIENTLY, EFFORTLESSLY, SILENTLY."
WHIT'S THAT, MAW? I CANNA HEAR YE FOR A' THE HUMMIN' AN' BUZZIN'!

Labour-saving devices can be a great help to the busy housewife.

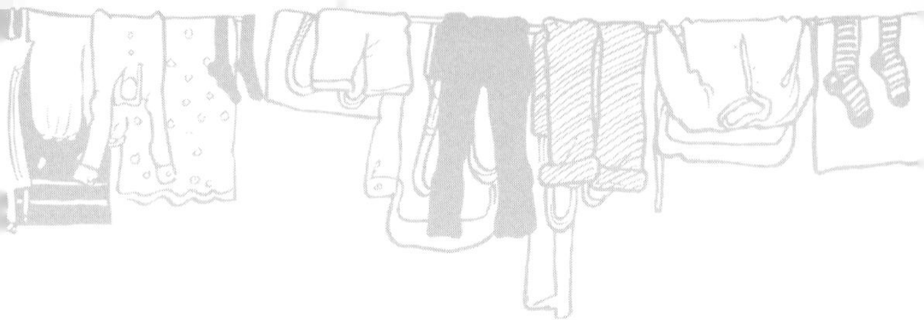

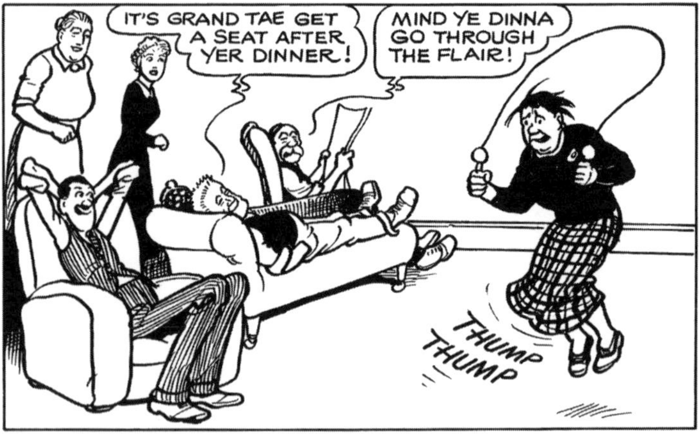
IT'S GRAND TAE GET A SEAT AFTER YER DINNER!
MIND YE DINNA GO THROUGH THE FLAIR!
THUMP THUMP

It is important to encourage self-improvement in others.

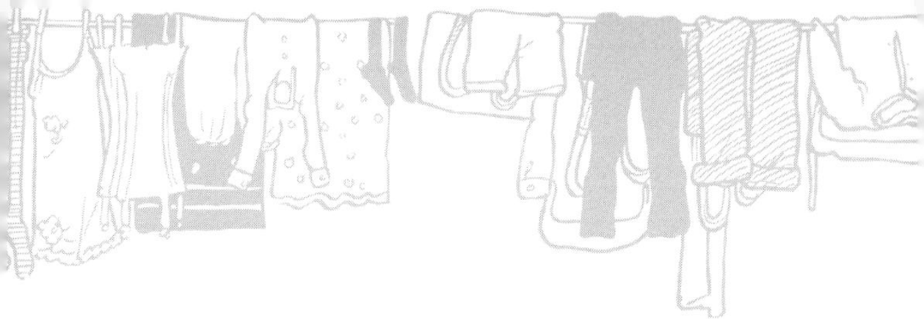

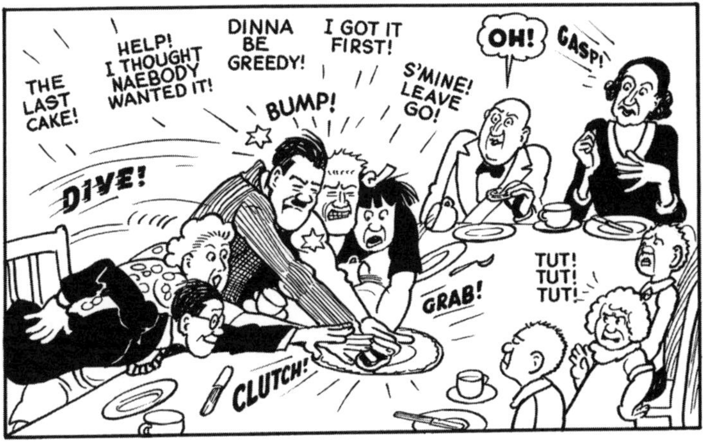
THE LAST CAKE!
HELP! I THOUGHT NAEBODY WANTED IT!
DINNA BE GREEDY!
I GOT IT FIRST!
OH!
GASP!
DIVE!
BUMP!
S'MINE! LEAVE GO!
GRAB!
TUT! TUT! TUT!
CLUTCH!

The power of good table manners should not be overestimated.

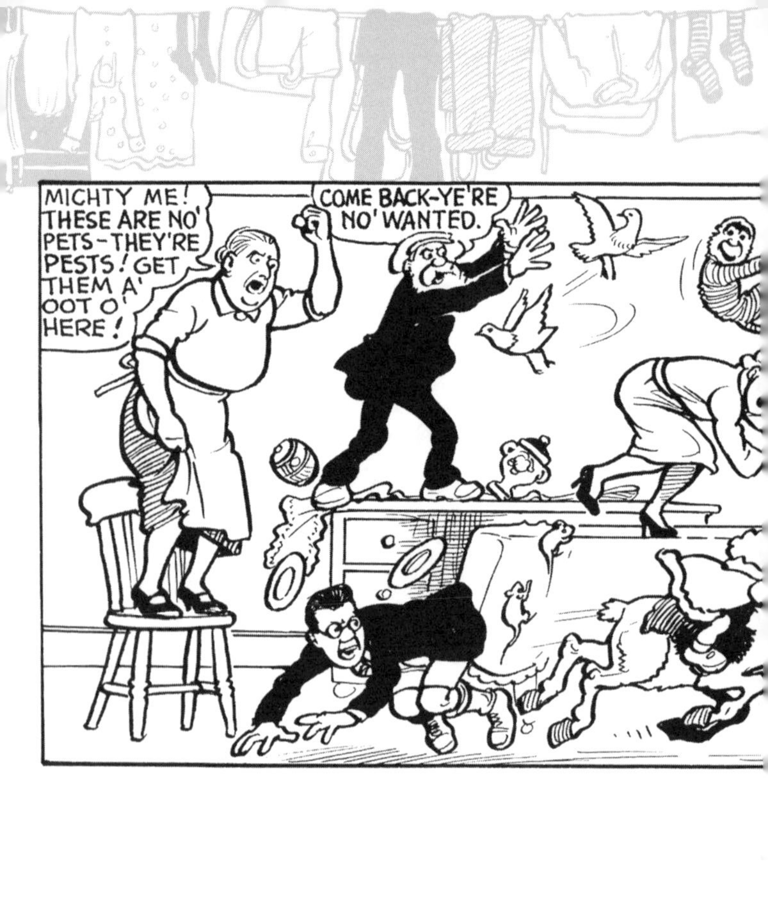
MICHTY ME! THESE ARE NO' PETS–THEY'RE PESTS! GET THEM A' OOT O' HERE!
COME BACK–YE'RE NO' WANTED.

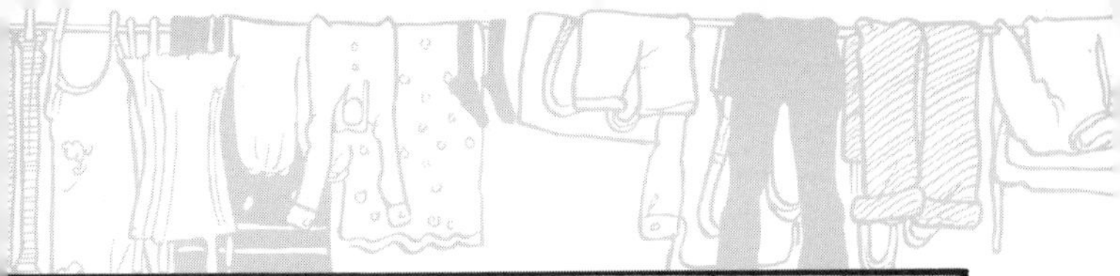

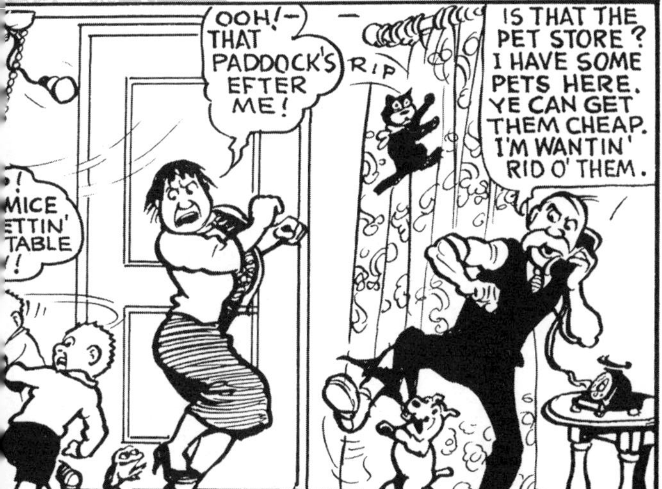
MICE
ETTIN'
TABLE
OOH!— THAT PADDOCK'S EFTER ME!
RIP
IS THAT THE PET STORE ? I HAVE SOME PETS HERE. YE CAN GET THEM CHEAP. I'M WANTIN' RID O' THEM.

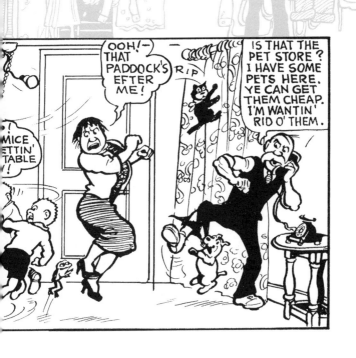

ets can provide excellent stress relief.

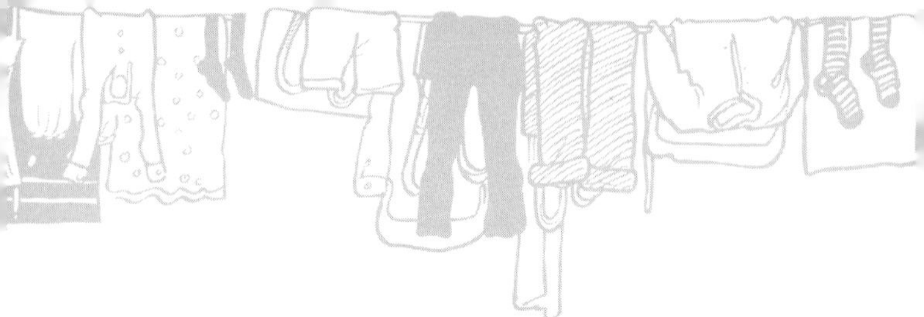

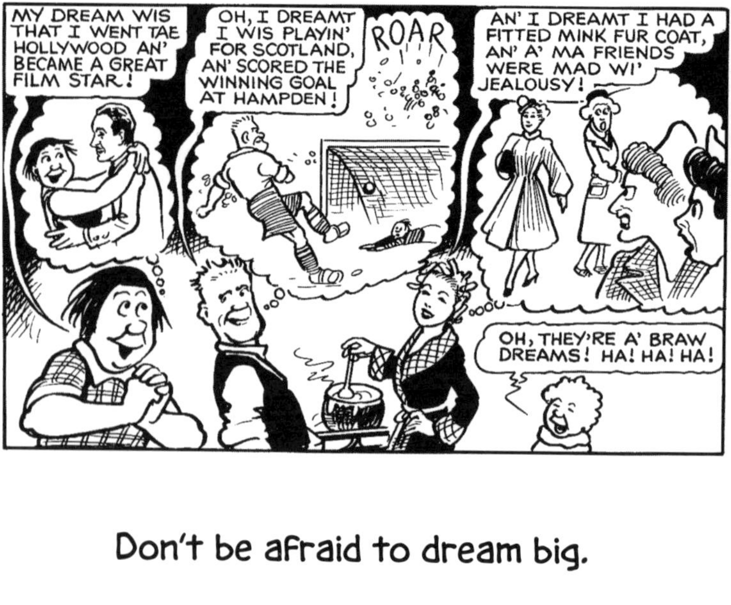
MY DREAM WIS THAT I WENT TAE HOLLYWOOD AN' BECAME A GREAT FILM STAR!
OH, I DREAMT I WIS PLAYIN' FOR SCOTLAND, AN' SCORED THE WINNING GOAL AT HAMPDEN!
ROAR
AN' I DREAMT I HAD A FITTED MINK FUR COAT, AN' A' MA FRIENDS WERE MAD WI' JEALOUSY!
OH, THEY'RE A' BRAW DREAMS! HA! HA! HA!

Don't be afraid to dream big.

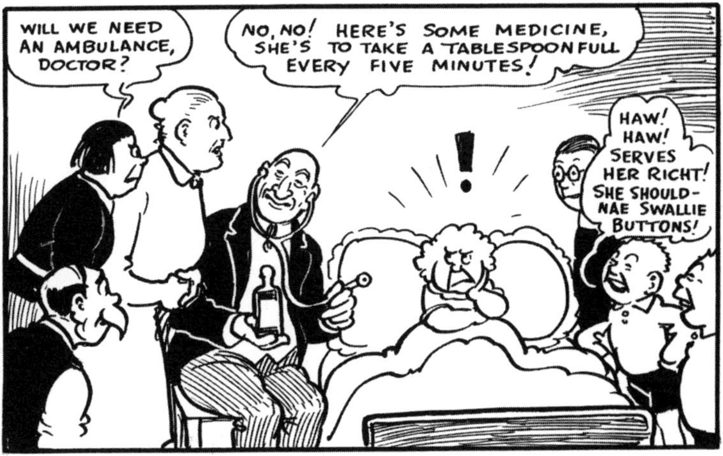
WILL WE NEED AN AMBULANCE, DOCTOR?
NO, NO! HERE'S SOME MEDICINE, SHE'S TO TAKE A TABLESPOONFULL EVERY FIVE MINUTES!
!
HAW! HAW! SERVES HER RICHT! SHE SHOULD-NAE SWALLIE BUTTONS!

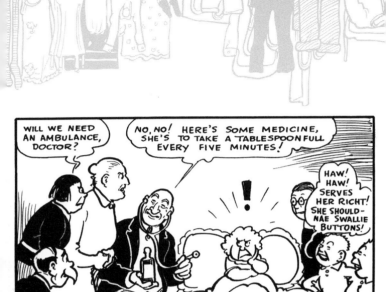

Sometimes you have to be
cruel to be kind.

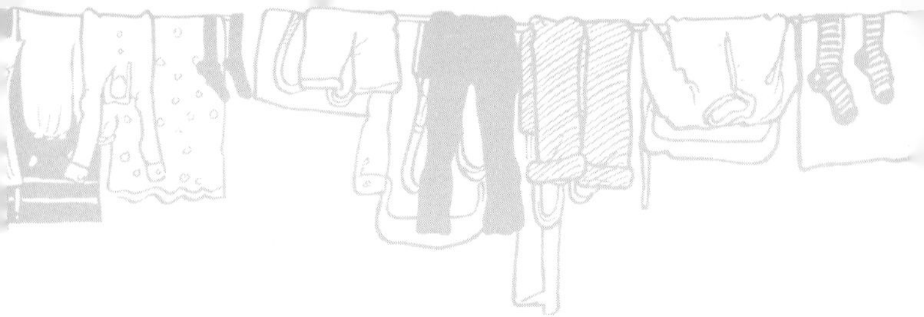

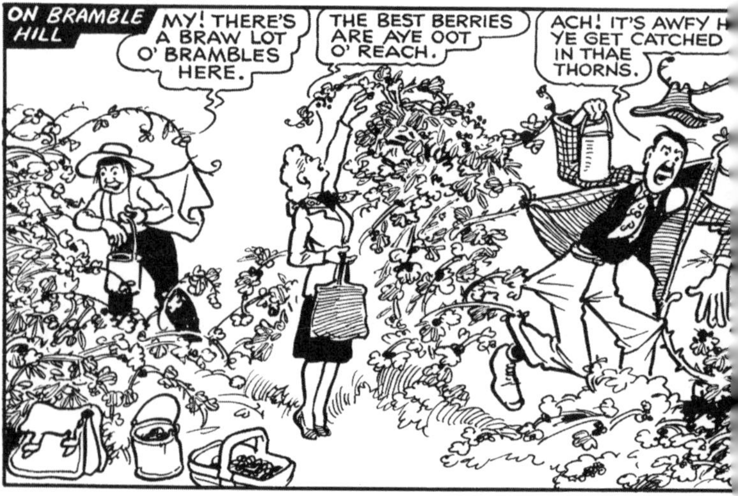
ON BRAMBLE HILL
MY! THERE'S A BRAW LOT O' BRAMBLES HERE.
THE BEST BERRIES ARE AYE OOT O' REACH.
ACH! IT'S AWFY YE GET CATCHED IN THAE THORNS.

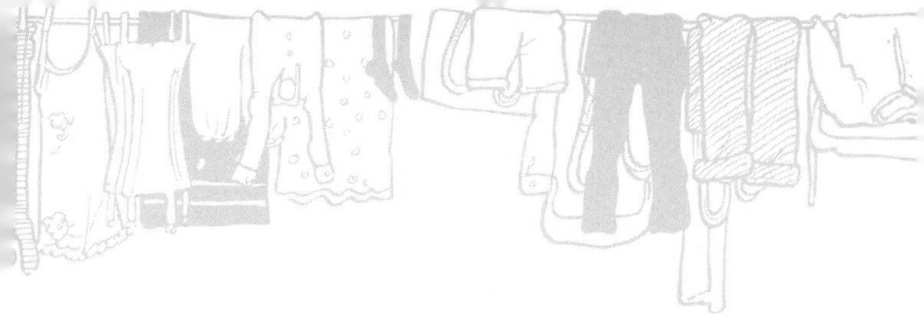

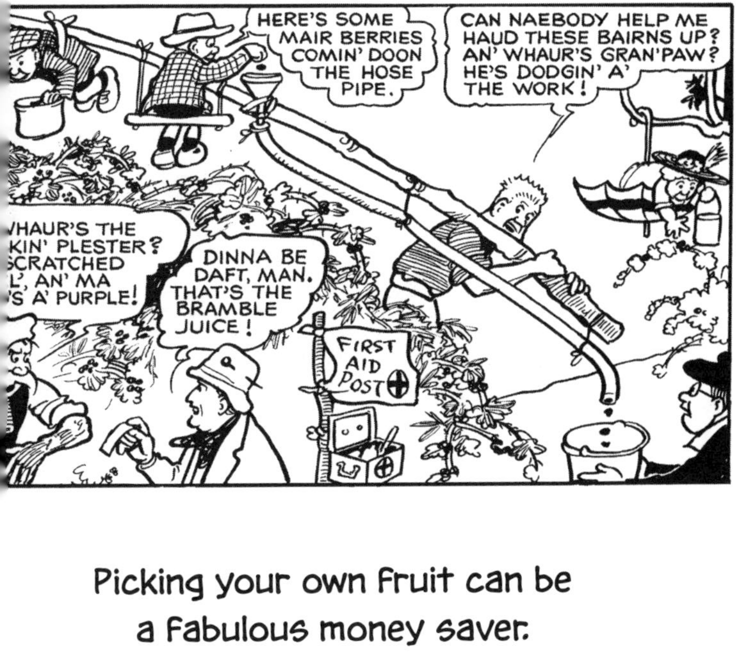
HERE'S SOME MAIR BERRIES COMIN' DOON THE HOSE PIPE.
CAN NAEBODY HELP ME HAUD THESE BAIRNS UP? AN' WHAUR'S GRAN'PAW? HE'S DODGIN' A' THE WORK!
HAUR'S THE KIN' PLESTER? CRATCHED L', AN' MA 'S A' PURPLE!
DINNA BE DAFT, MAN. THAT'S THE BRAMBLE JUICE!
FIRST AID POST

Picking your own fruit can be a fabulous money saver.

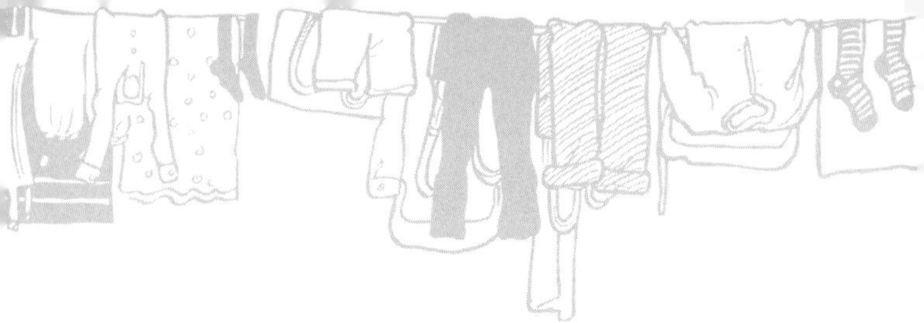

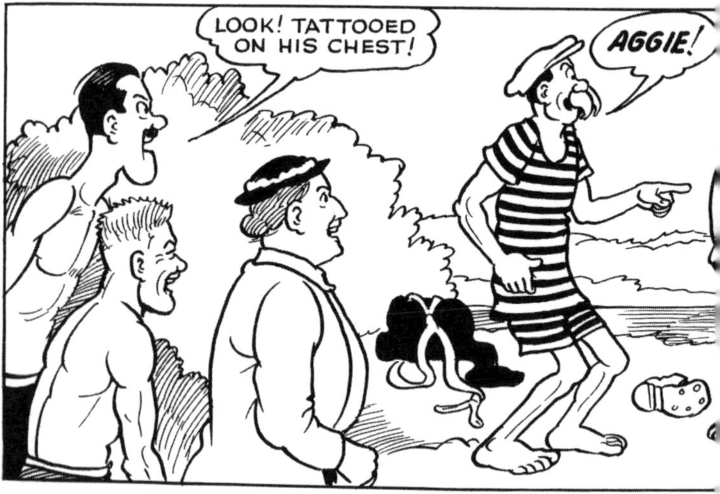
LOOK! TATTOOED ON HIS CHEST!
AGGIE!

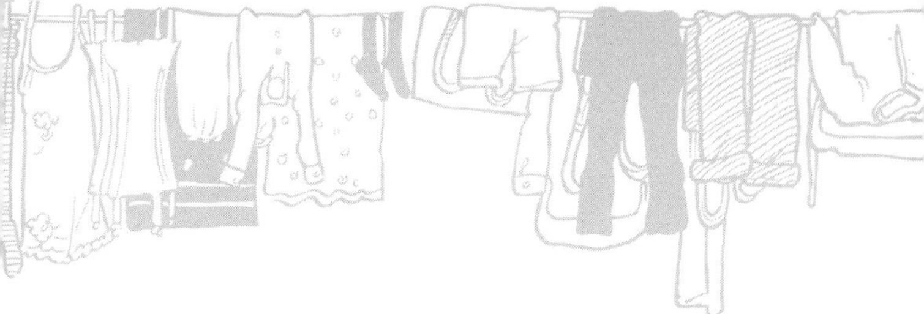

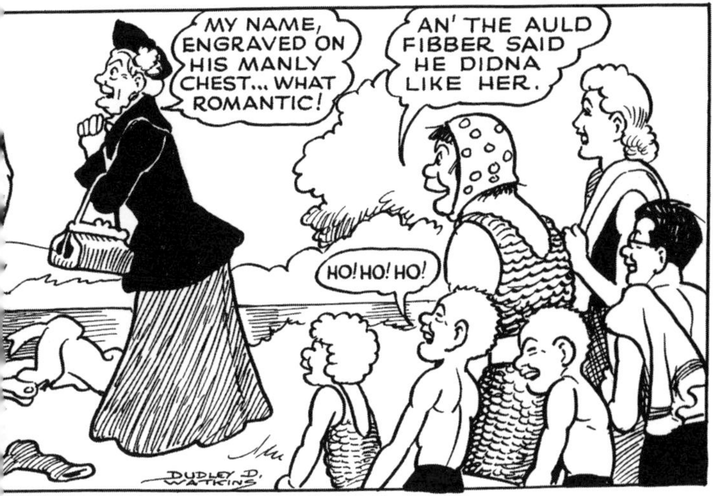
MY NAME, ENGRAVED ON HIS MANLY CHEST... WHAT ROMANTIC!
AN' THE AULD FIBBER SAID HE DIDNA LIKE HER.
HO! HO! HO!
DUDLEY D. WATKINS

Beware! Mistakes of the past will always catch up with you eventually.

IT'S NO' MRS McGIBBON'S GRANNY THAT'S NEEDIN' BANDAGED, IT'S OOR AIN FAITHER GOT TRAMPLED ON GOIN' DOON THE STAIR!
W-WHIT HAVE I DONE TAE DESERVE THIS?
FIRST AID
DUDLEY D. WATKINS

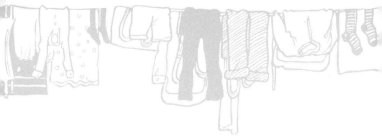

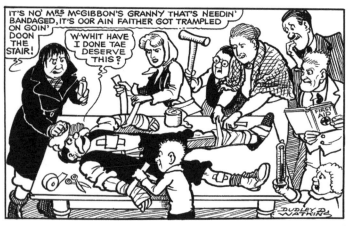

A good grounding in
first aid is essential.

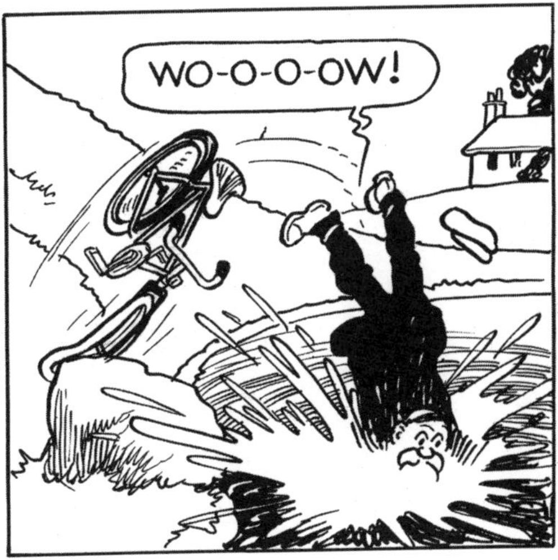
WO-O-O-OW!

Cycling and Swimming make excellent forms of exercise.

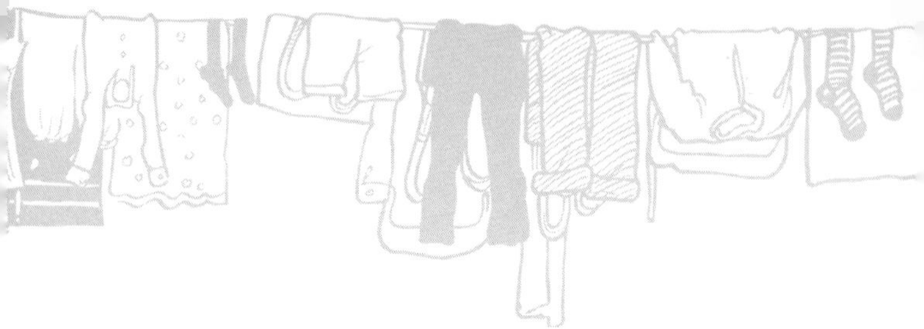

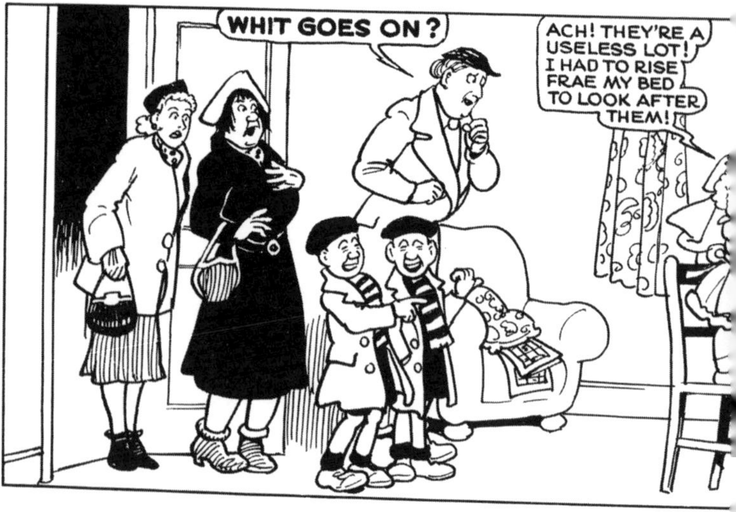

WHIT GOES ON?
ACH! THEY'RE A USELESS LOT! I HAD TO RISE FRAE MY BED TO LOOK AFTER THEM!

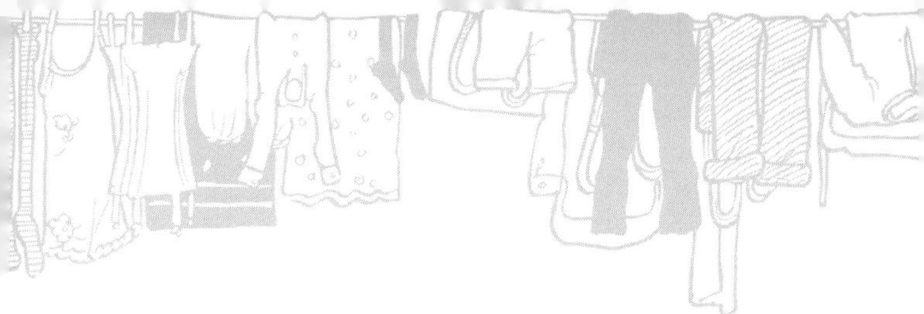

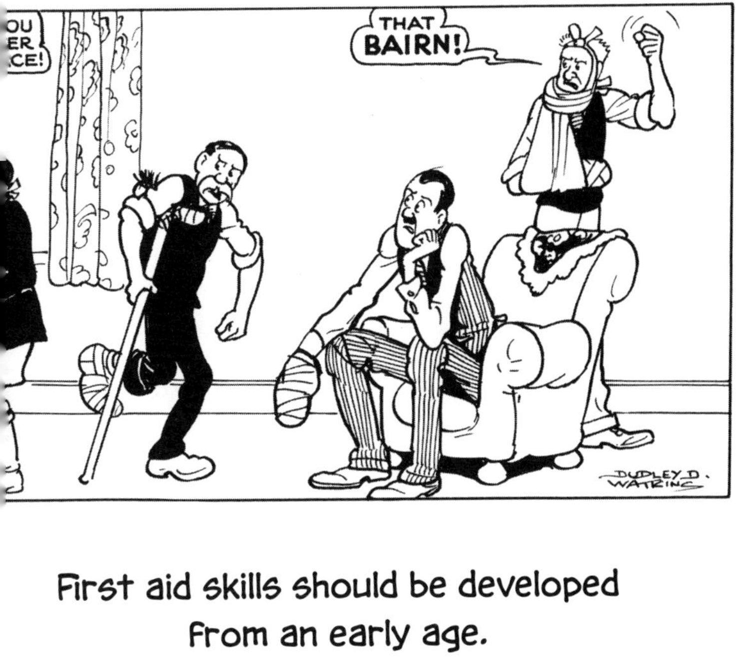
THAT BAIRN!
DUDLEY D. WATKINS

First aid skills should be developed from an early age.

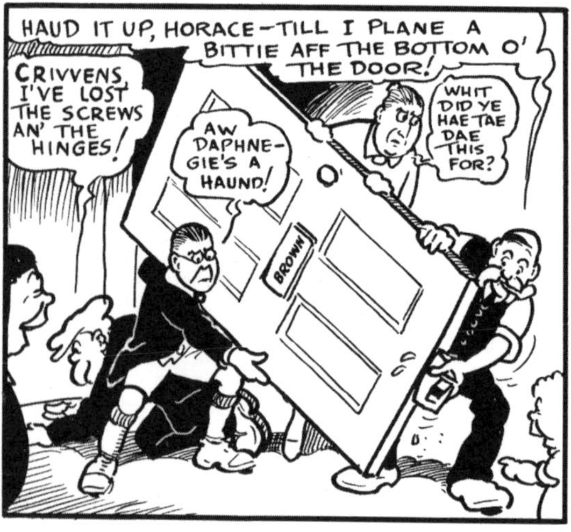
HAUD IT UP, HORACE—TILL I PLANE A BITTIE AFF THE BOTTOM O' THE DOOR!
CRIVVENS, I'VE LOST THE SCREWS AN' THE HINGES!
AW DAPHNE-GIE'S A HAUND!
WHIT DID YE HAE TAE DAE THIS FOR?
BROWN

Sometimes it pays to bring in a professional.

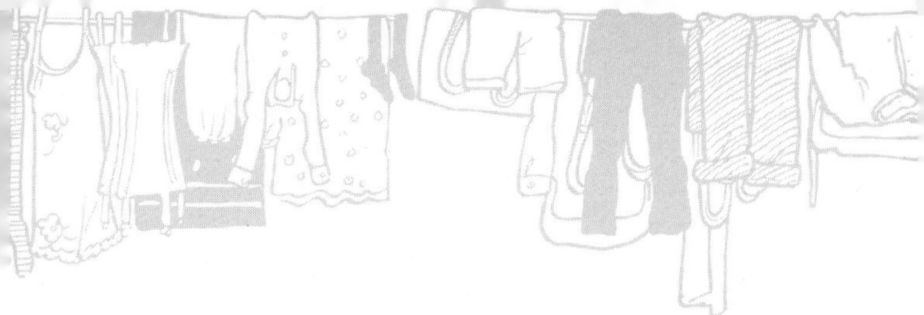

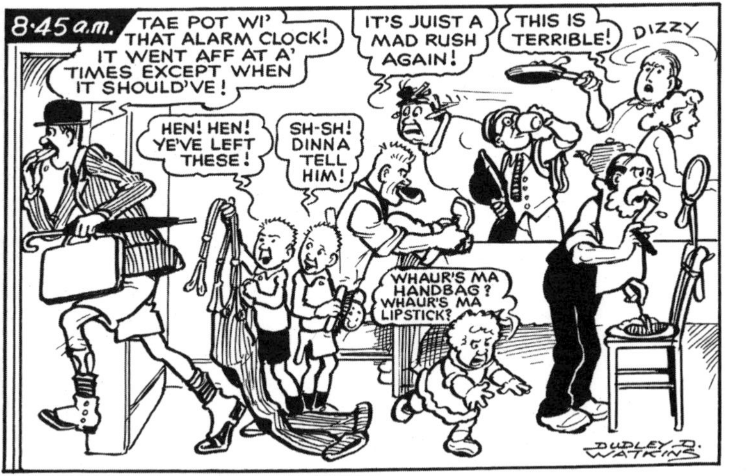
8·45 a.m.
TAE POT WI' THAT ALARM CLOCK! IT WENT AFF AT A' TIMES EXCEPT WHEN IT SHOULD'VE!
IT'S JUIST A MAD RUSH AGAIN!
THIS IS TERRIBLE!
DIZZY
HEN! HEN! YE'VE LEFT THESE!
SH-SH! DINNA TELL HIM!
WHAUR'S MA HANDBAG? WHAUR'S MA LIPSTICK?
DUDLEY D. WATKINS

Try setting an alarm clock if your family are not well organised.

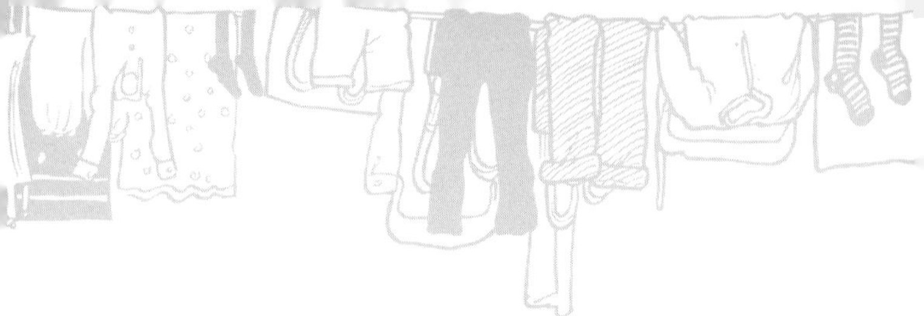

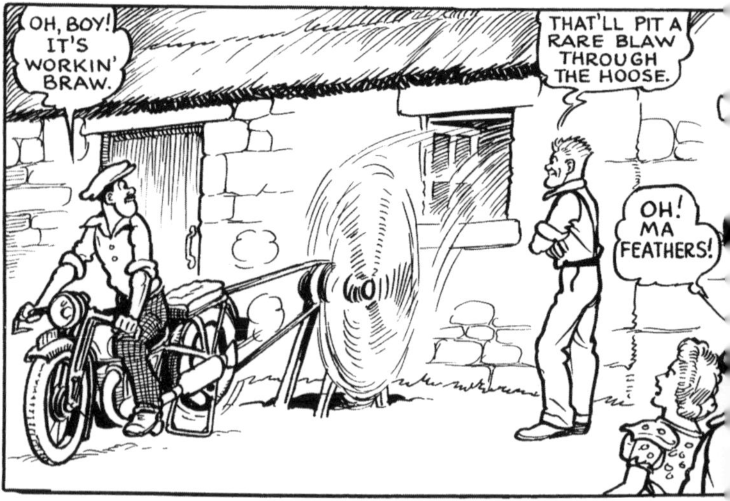
OH, BOY! IT'S WORKIN' BRAW.
THAT'LL PIT A RARE BLAW THROUGH THE HOOSE.
OH! MA FEATHERS!

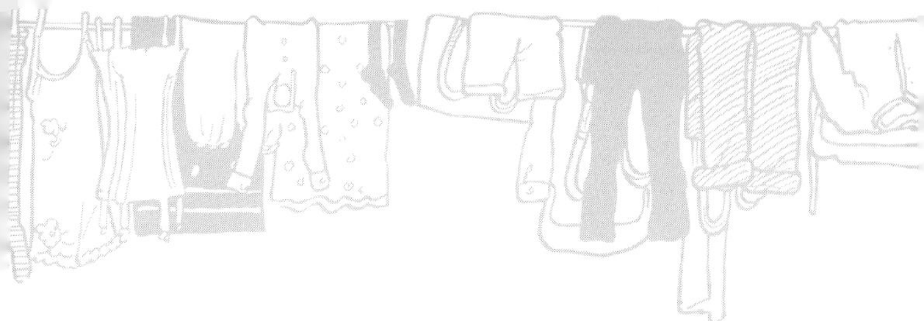

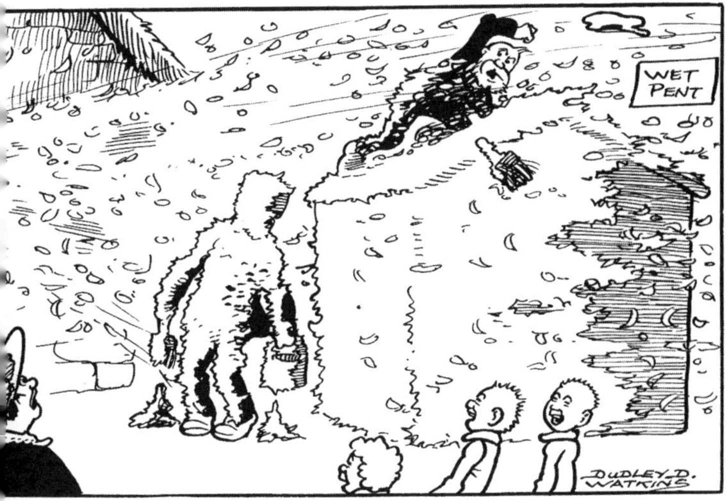
WET PENT
DUDLEY D. WATKINS

Stick to one home improvement at a time.

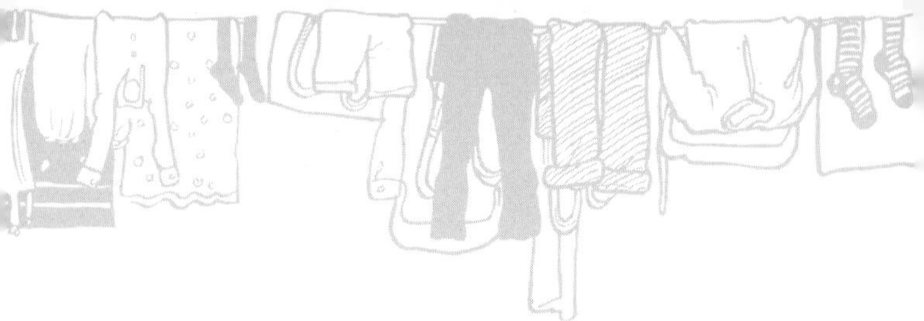

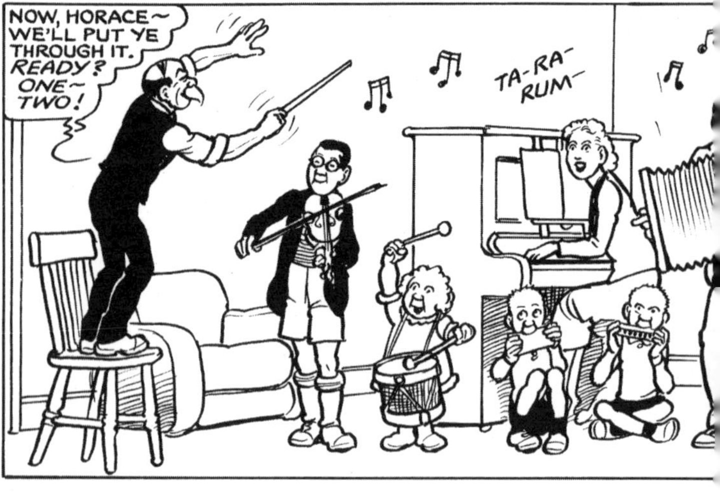
NOW, HORACE~ WE'LL PUT YE THROUGH IT. *READY? ONE~ TWO!*
TA-RA-RUM-

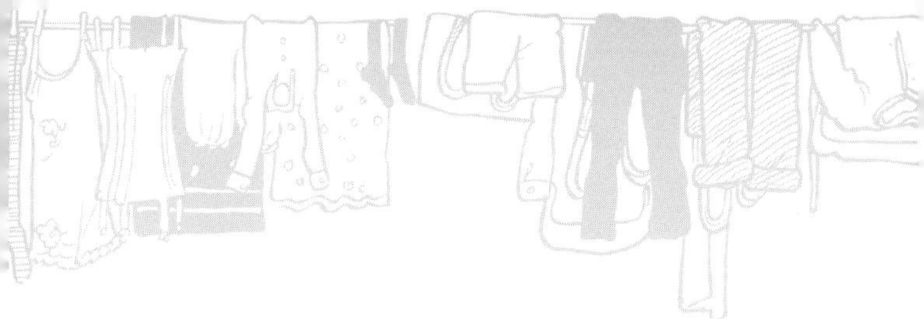

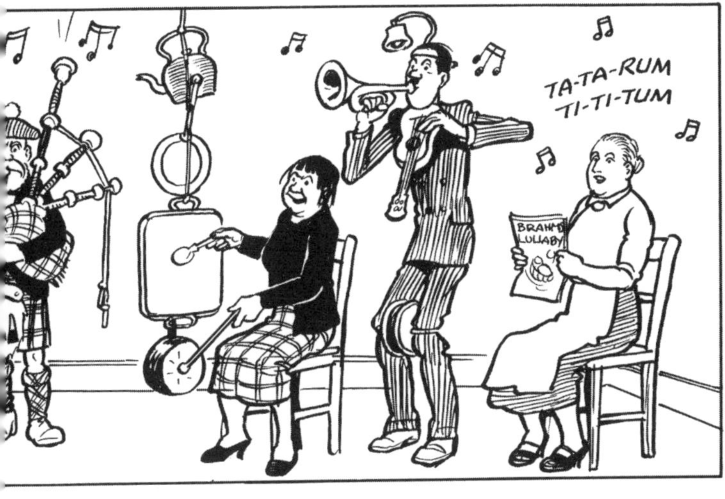
TA-TA-RUM
TI-TI-TUM
LULLABY

A home entertainment system will keep the whole family amused for hours.

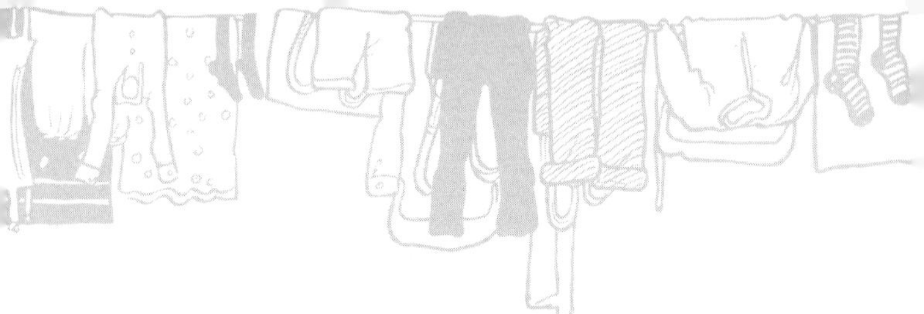

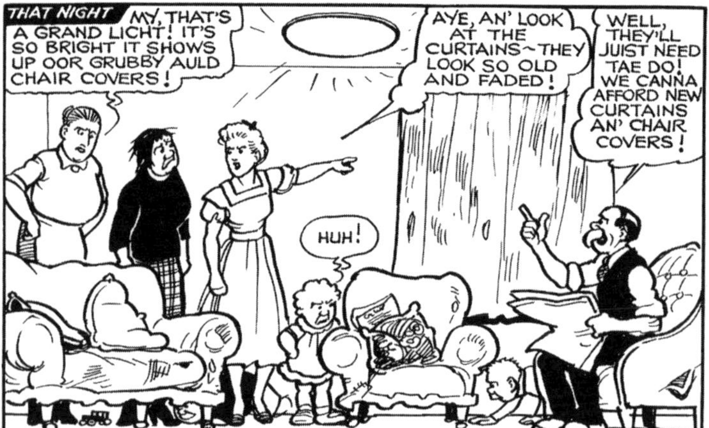
THAT NIGHT
MY, THAT'S A GRAND LICHT! IT'S SO BRIGHT IT SHOWS UP OOR GRUBBY AULD CHAIR COVERS!
AYE, AN' LOOK AT THE CURTAINS~THEY LOOK SO OLD AND FADED!
WELL, THEY'LL JUIST NEED TAE DO! WE CANNA AFFORD NEW CURTAINS AN' CHAIR COVERS!
HUH!

A dimly lit room hides
a multitude of sins.

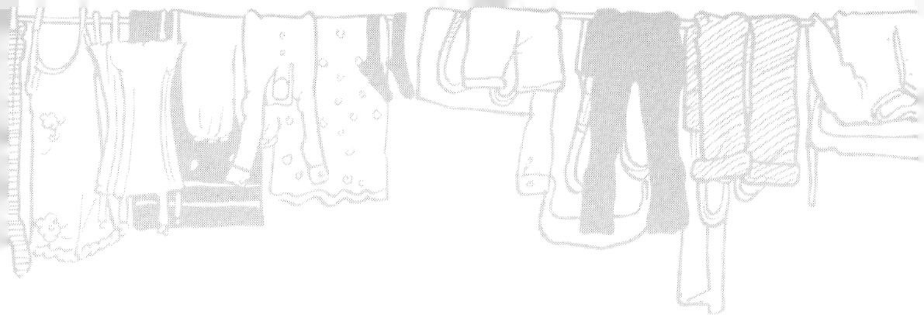

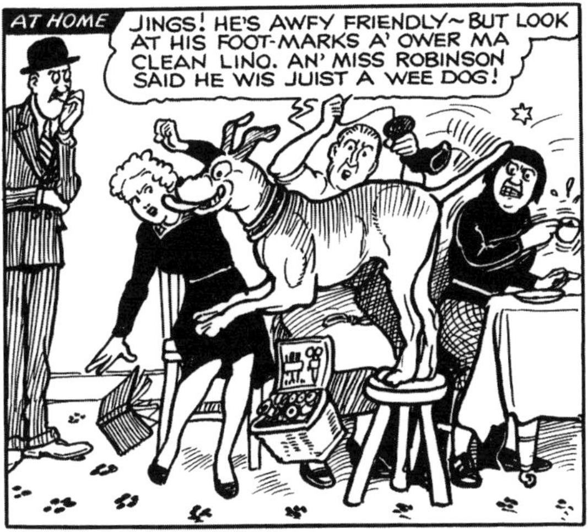
AT HOME
JINGS! HE'S AWFY FRIENDLY~ BUT LOOK AT HIS FOOT-MARKS A' OWER MA CLEAN LINO. AN' MISS ROBINSON SAID HE WIS JUIST A WEE DOG!

It is important to keep pets under control.

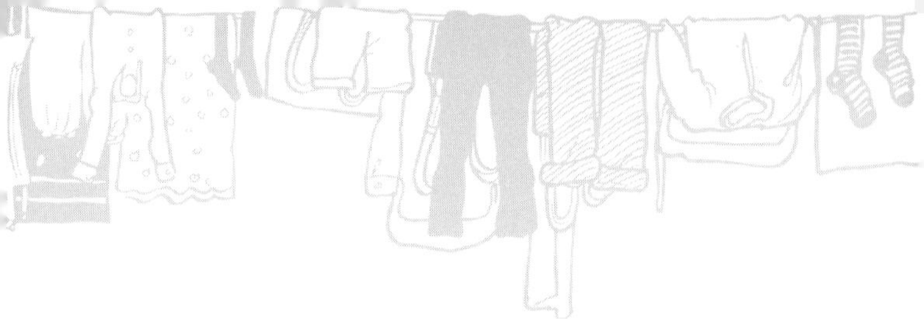

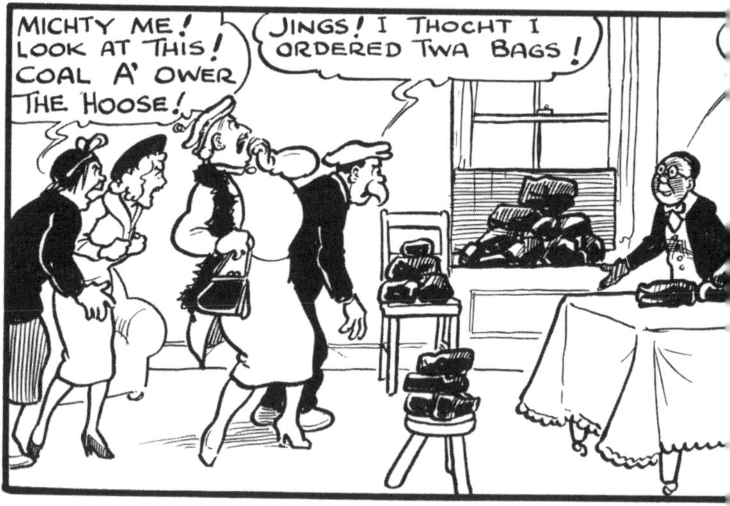
MICHTY ME! LOOK AT THIS! COAL A' OWER THE HOOSE!
JINGS! I THOCHT I ORDERED TWA BAGS!

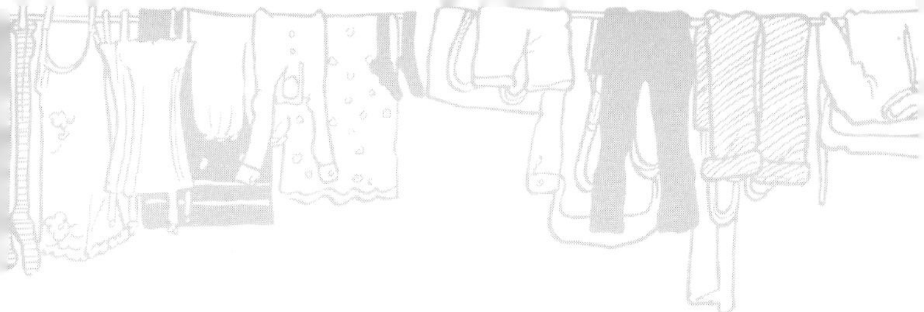

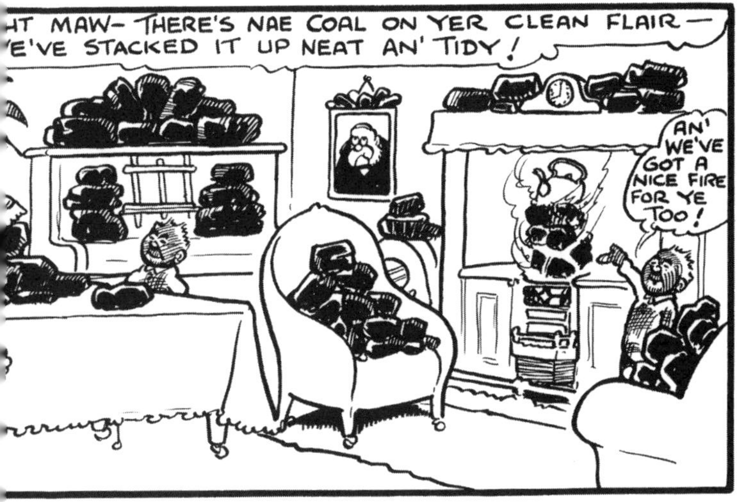
HT MAW– THERE'S NAE COAL ON YER CLEAN FLAIR—
'E'VE STACKED IT UP NEAT AN' TIDY!
AN' WE'VE GOT A NICE FIRE FOR YE TOO!

Always keep your living room neat and tidy.

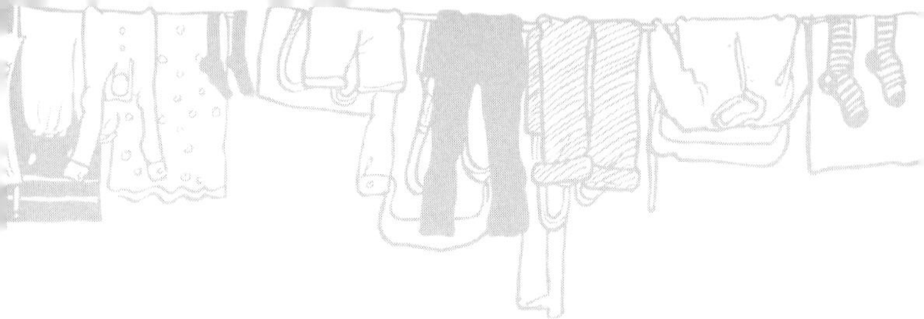

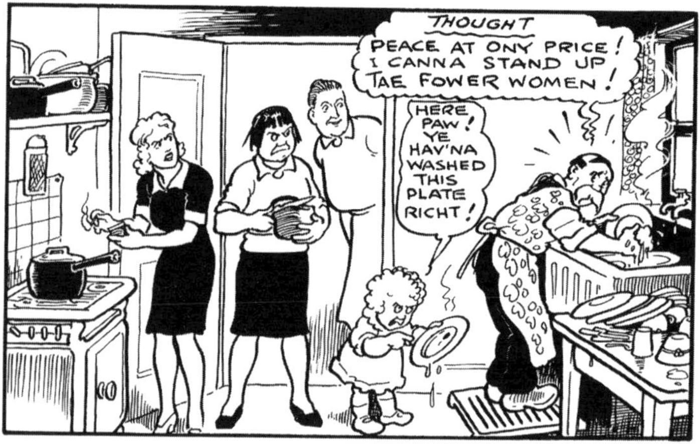
THOUGHT
PEACE AT ONY PRICE! I CANNA STAND UP TAE FOWER WOMEN!
HERE, PAW! YE HAV'NA WASHED THIS PLATE RICHT!

Allow the man of the house
to share the workload.

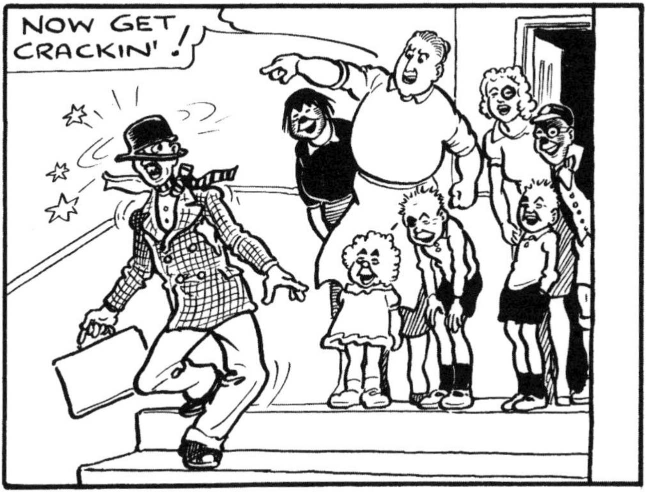
NOW GET CRACKIN' !

Never mess with
Maw Broon's family . . . EVER!

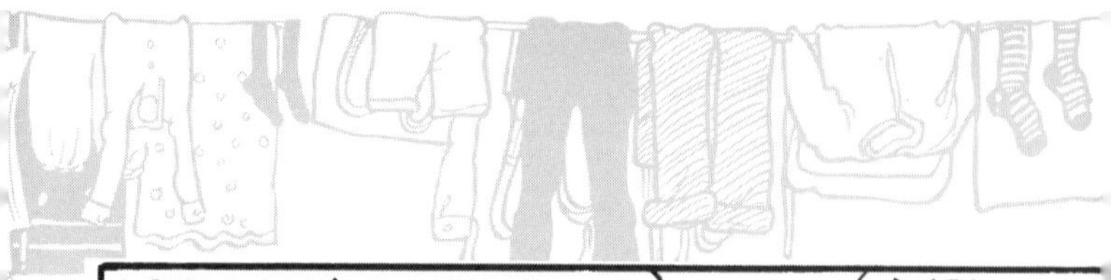

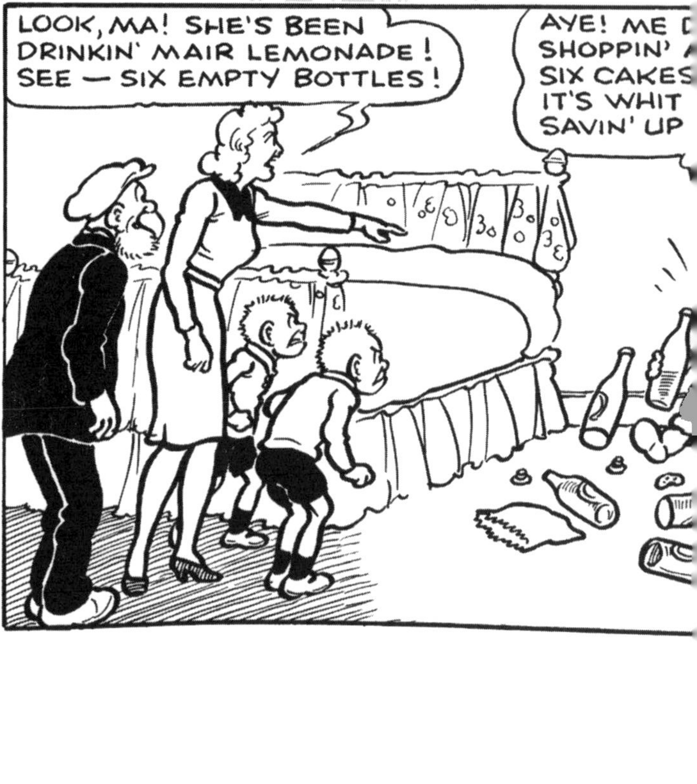
LOOK, MA! SHE'S BEEN DRINKIN' MAIR LEMONADE! SEE — SIX EMPTY BOTTLES!
AYE! ME
SHOPPIN'
SIX CAKES
IT'S WHIT
SAVIN' UP

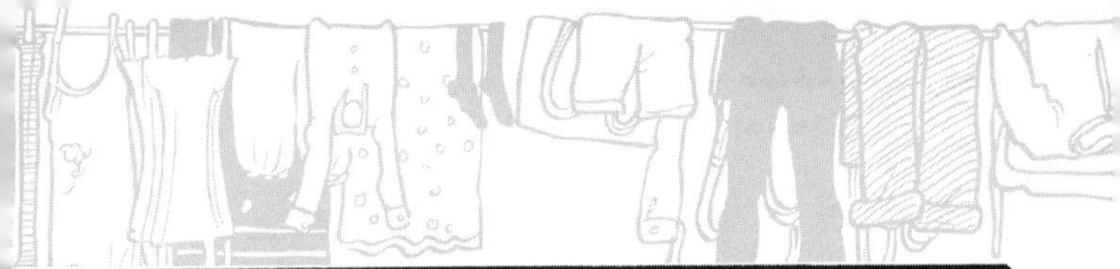

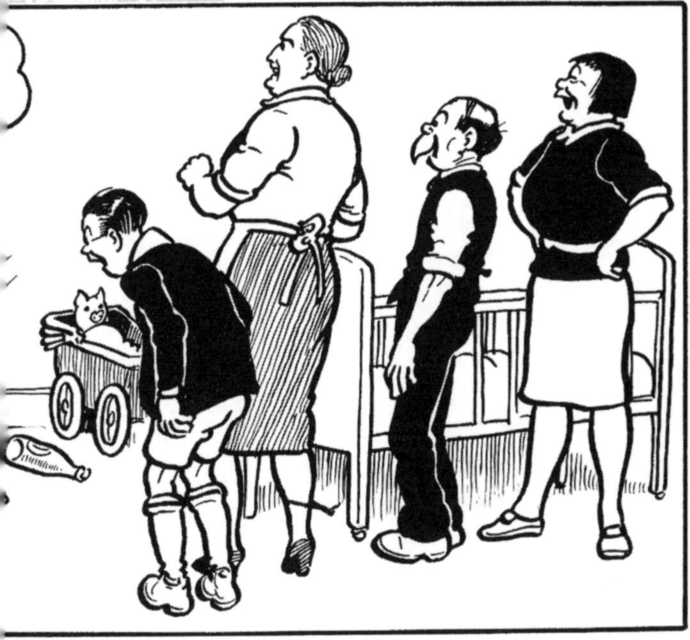

Encourage healthy eating
from an early age.

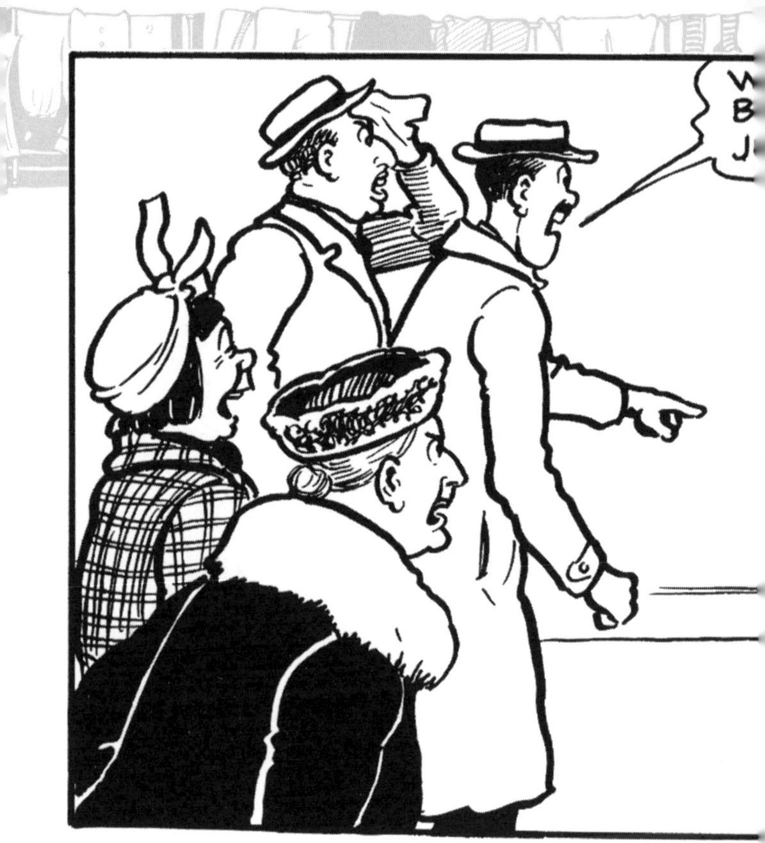

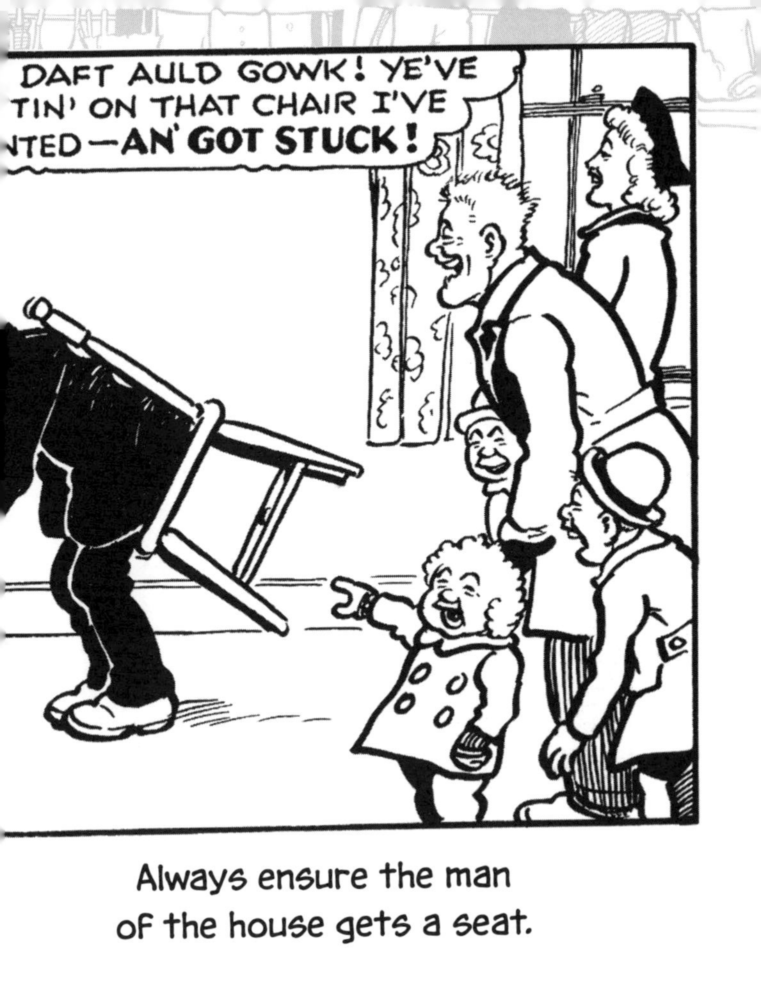
DAFT AULD GOWK! YE'VE
TIN' ON THAT CHAIR I'VE
NTED—AN' GOT STUCK!

Always ensure the man
of the house gets a seat.

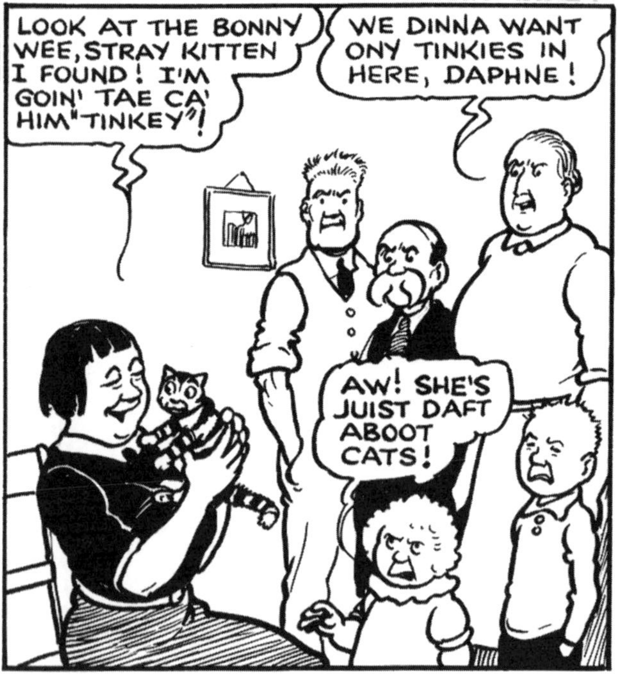
LOOK AT THE BONNY WEE, STRAY KITTEN I FOUND! I'M GOIN' TAE CA' HIM "TINKEY"!
WE DINNA WANT ONY TINKIES IN HERE, DAPHNE!
AW! SHE'S JUIST DAFT ABOOT CATS!

Be careful when selecting pet names.

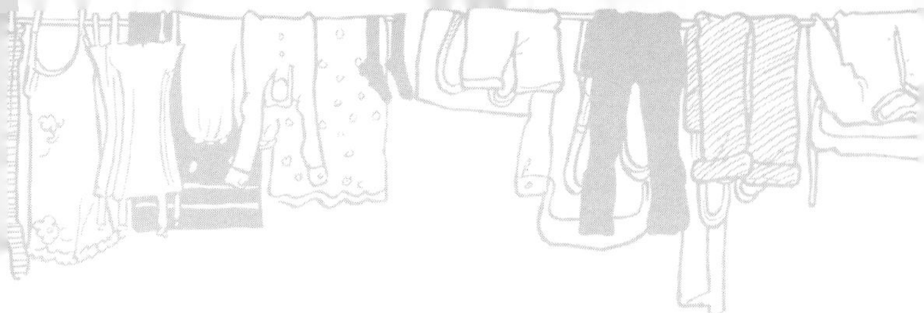

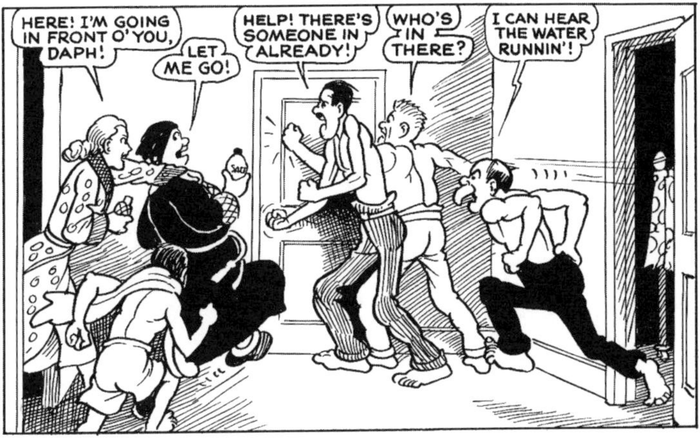

HERE! I'M GOING IN FRONT O' YOU, DAPH!
LET ME GO!
HELP! THERE'S SOMEONE IN ALREADY!
WHO'S IN THERE?
I CAN HEAR THE WATER RUNNIN'!

Setting up a bathroom rota will prevent problems in the mornings.

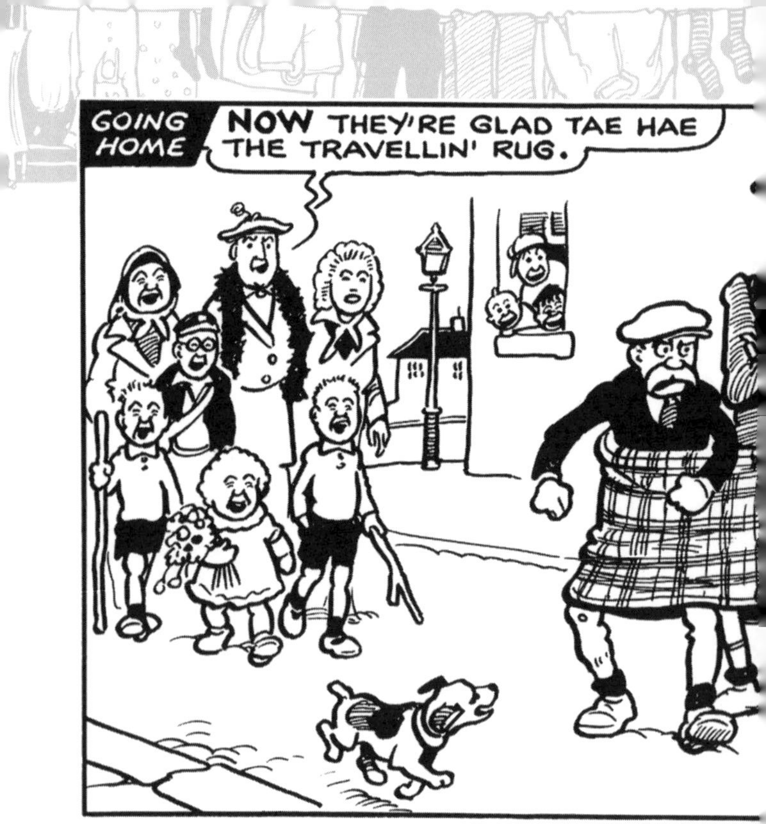
GOING HOME
NOW THEY'RE GLAD TAE HAE THE TRAVELLIN' RUG.

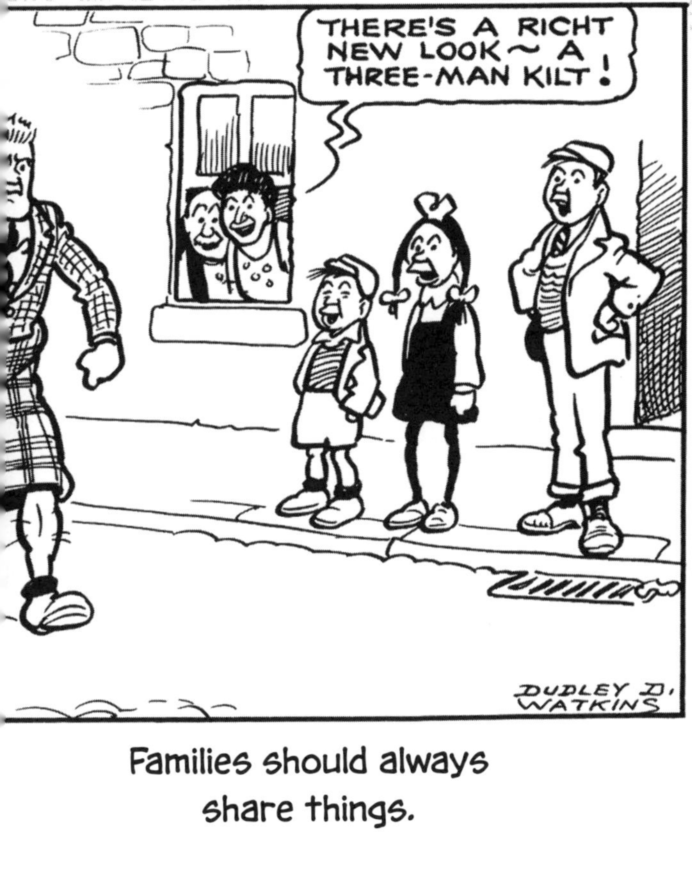
THERE'S A RICHT NEW LOOK ~ A THREE-MAN KILT!
DUDLEY D. WATKINS

Families should always share things.

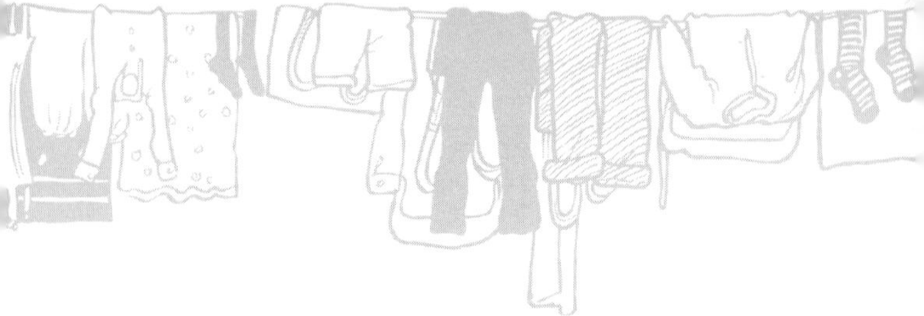

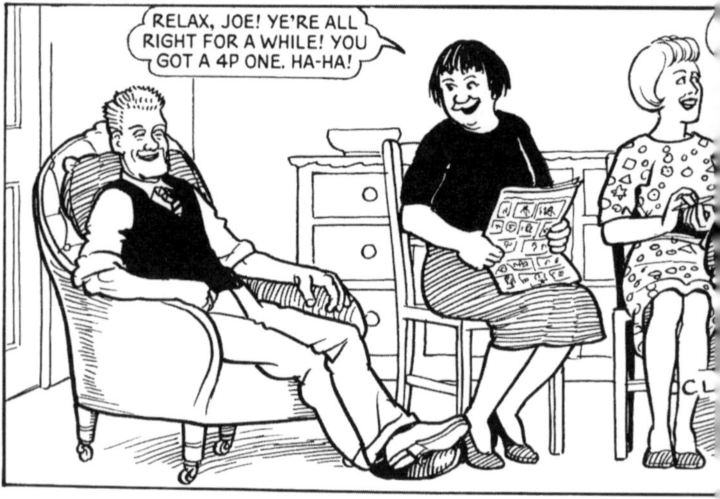
RELAX, JOE! YE'RE ALL RIGHT FOR A WHILE! YOU GOT A 4P ONE. HA-HA!

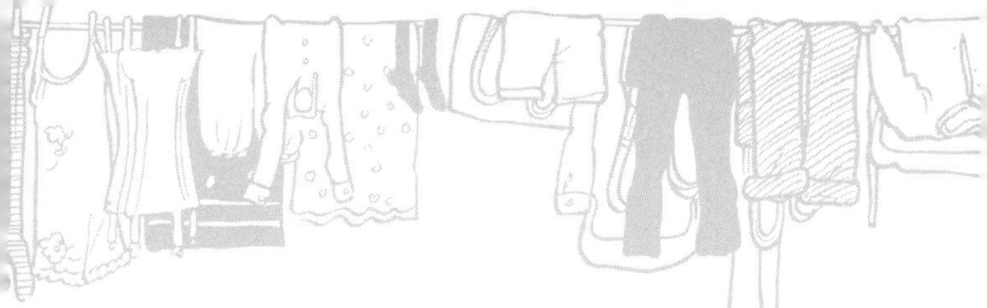

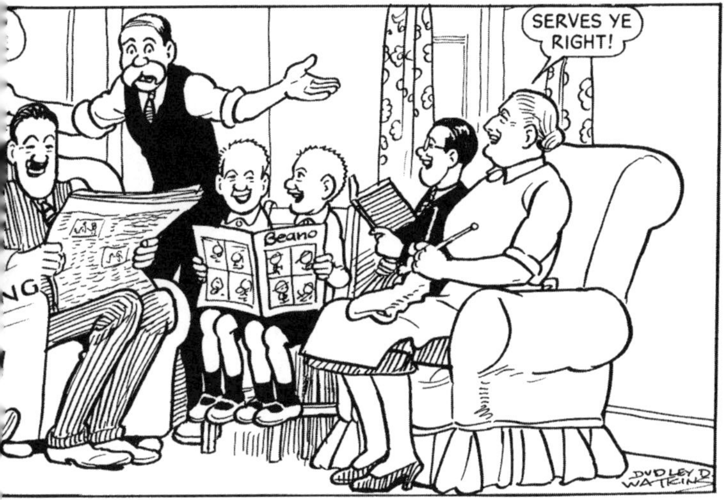
SERVES YE RIGHT!
Beano
DUDLEY D. WATKINS

It's never too early to plan a future career.

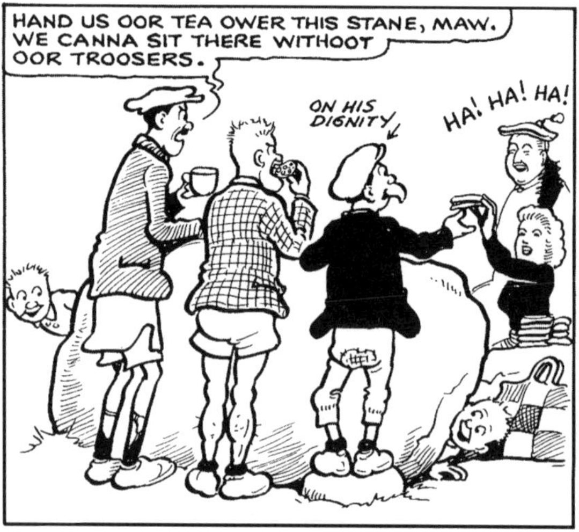
HAND US OOR TEA OWER THIS STANE, MAW. WE CANNA SIT THERE WITHOOT OOR TROOSERS.
ON HIS DIGNITY
HA! HA! HA!

It's important to keep your dignity in all situations.

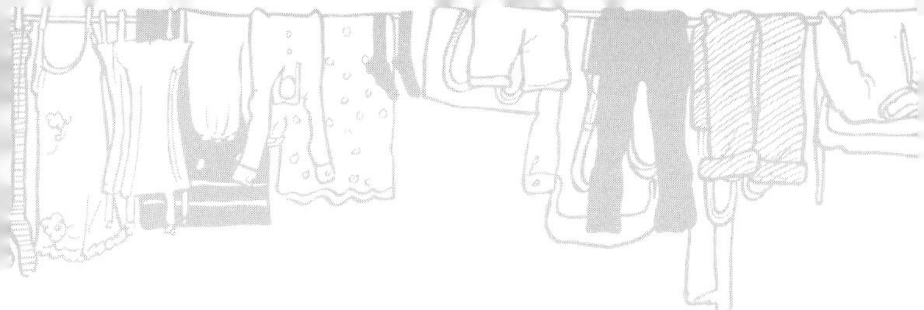

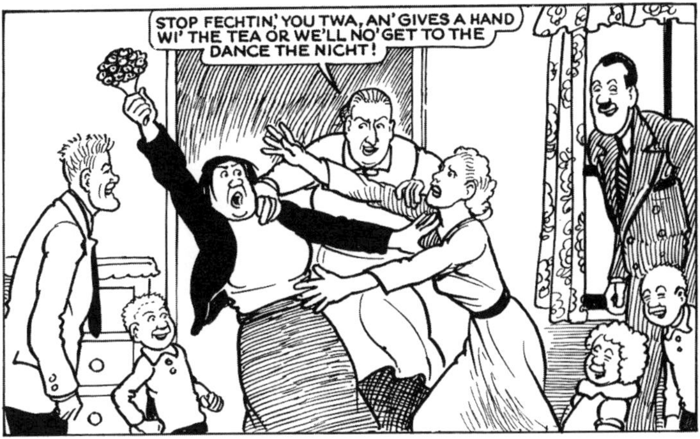
STOP FECHTIN,' YOU TWA, AN' GIVES A HAND WI' THE TEA OR WE'LL NO' GET TO THE DANCE THE NICHT!

Disputes should always
be settled amicably.

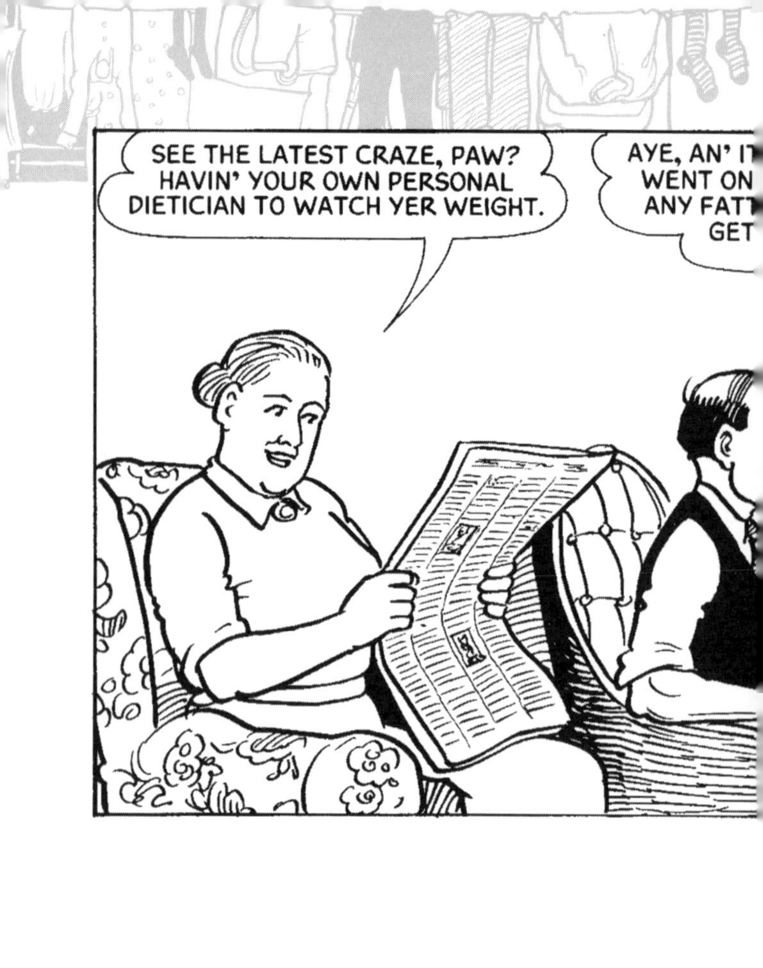
SEE THE LATEST CRAZE, PAW? HAVIN' YOUR OWN PERSONAL DIETICIAN TO WATCH YER WEIGHT.
AYE, AN' I
WENT ON
ANY FATT
GET

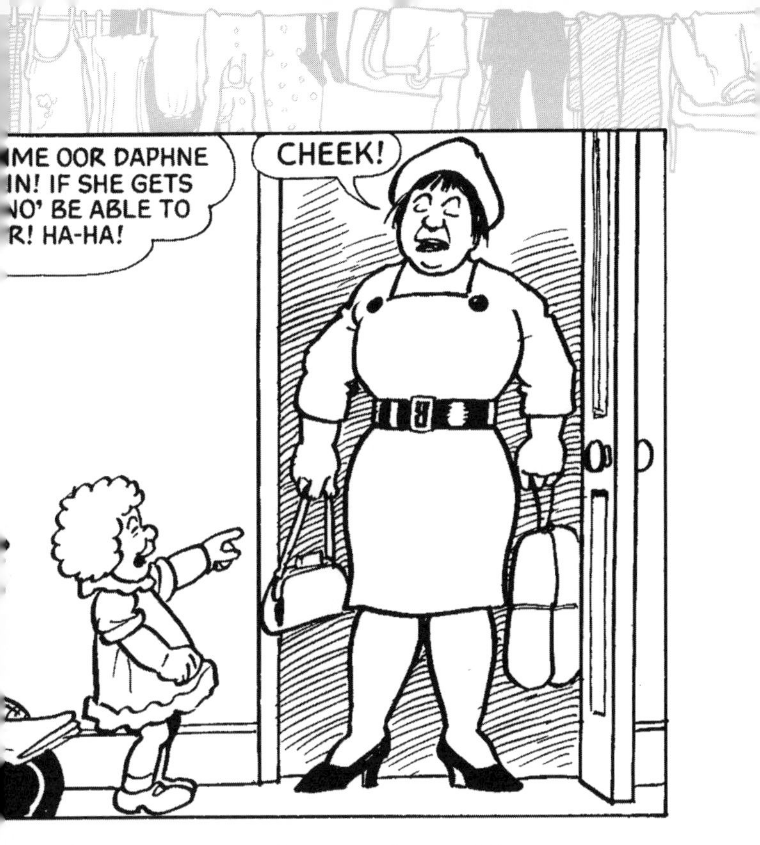
IME OOR DAPHNE
IN! IF SHE GETS
NO' BE ABLE TO
R! HA-HA!
CHEEK!

Always be polite and positive when making personal remarks.

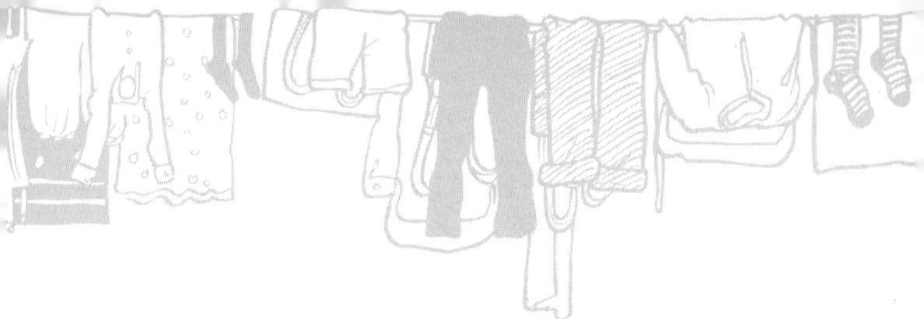

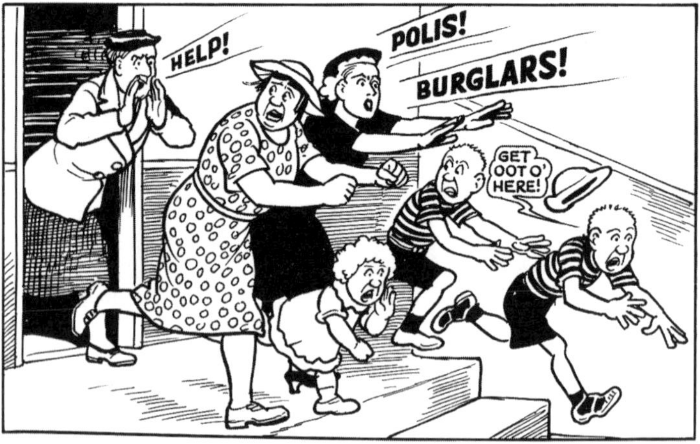
HELP!
POLIS!
BURGLARS!
GET OOT O' HERE!

Whatever happens, do not panic!

IT'S THESE BROONS AGAIN!
DUDLEY D. WATKINS

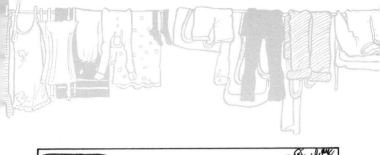

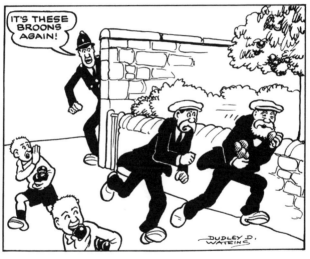

The elders of the family should set a good example.

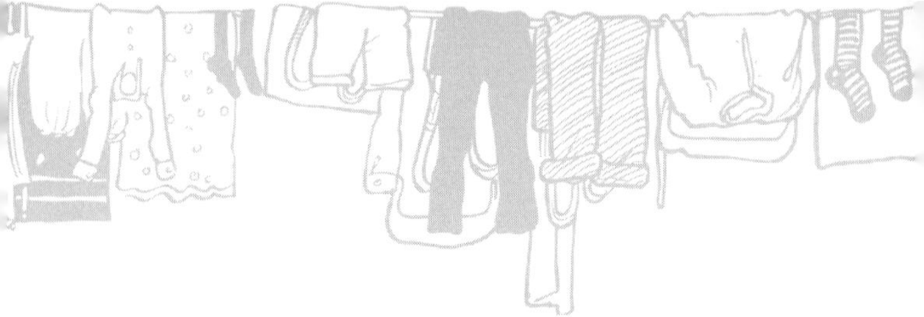

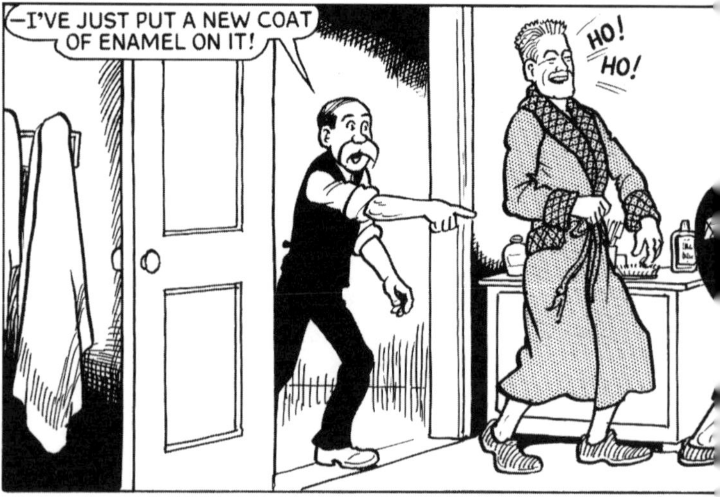
—I'VE JUST PUT A NEW COAT OF ENAMEL ON IT!
HO! HO!

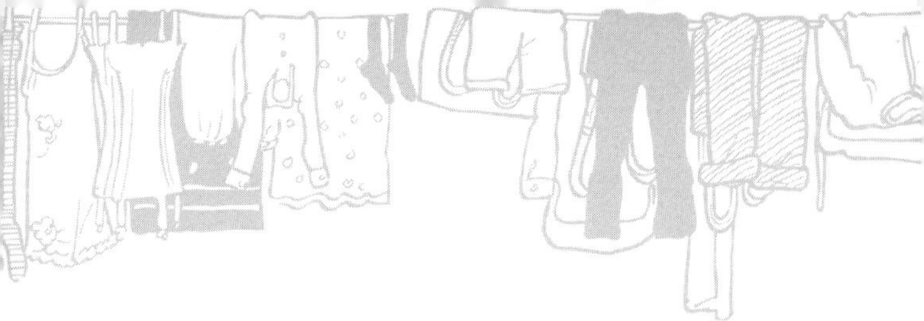

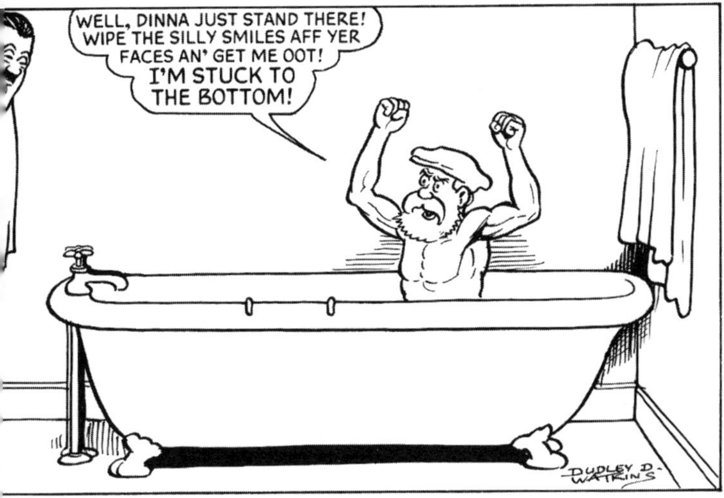
WELL, DINNA JUST STAND THERE! WIPE THE SILLY SMILES AFF YER FACES AN' GET ME OOT! I'M STUCK TO THE BOTTOM!
DUDLEY D. WATKINS

Don't spend too long in the bath.

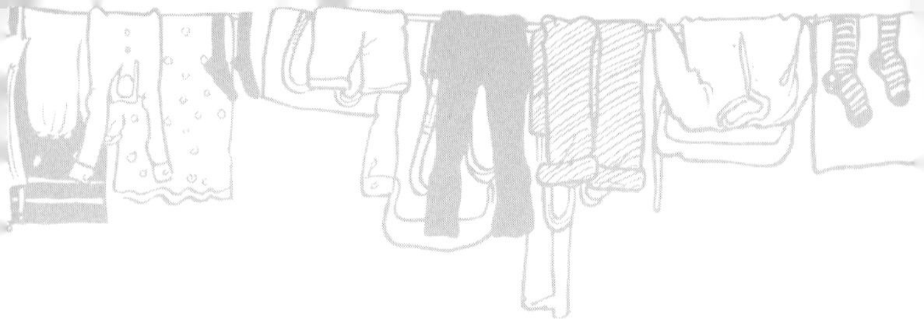

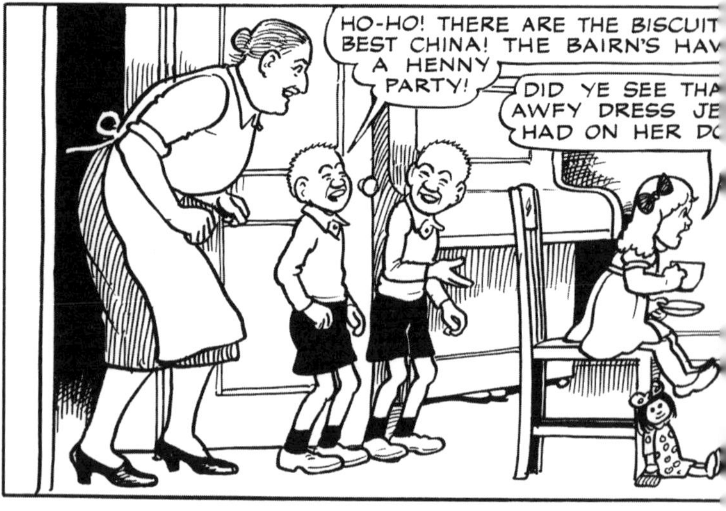
HO-HO! THERE ARE THE BISCUIT
BEST CHINA! THE BAIRN'S HAV
A HENNY PARTY!
DID YE SEE THA
AWFY DRESS JE
HAD ON HER D

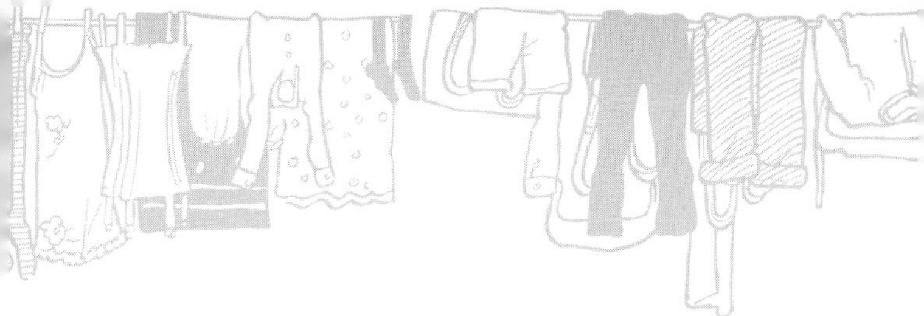

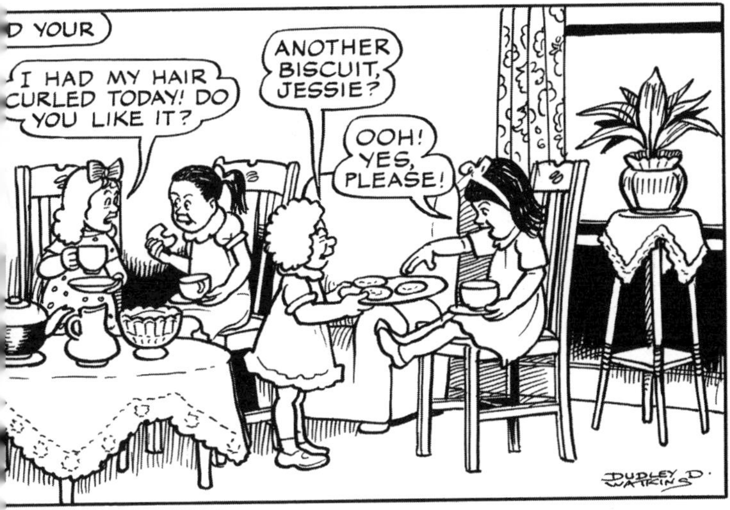

D YOUR
I HAD MY HAIR CURLED TODAY! DO YOU LIKE IT?
ANOTHER BISCUIT, JESSIE?
OOH! YES, PLEASE!
DUDLEY D. WATKINS

Remember that young children
can be impressionable.

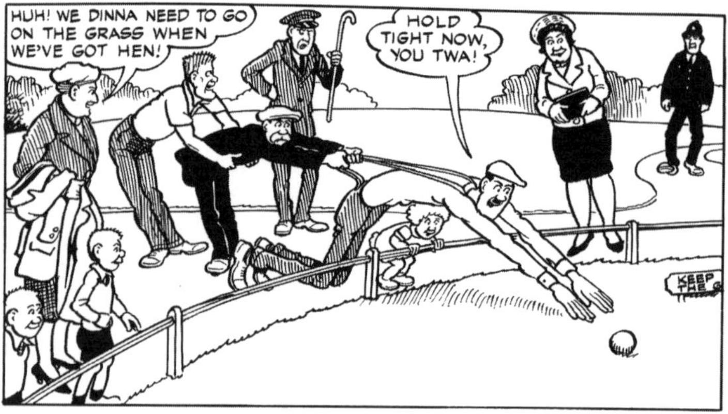
HUH! WE DINNA NEED TO GO ON THE GRASS WHEN WE'VE GOT HEN!
HOLD TIGHT NOW, YOU TWA!
KEEP THE

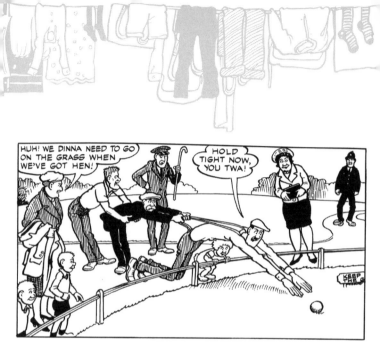

Do not break rules – bend them!

MICHTY! LOOK AT HIM! HE'S LETTIN' ON HE DOESN'T SEE US!
ILL-MANNERED SCUNNER!

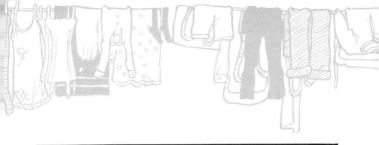

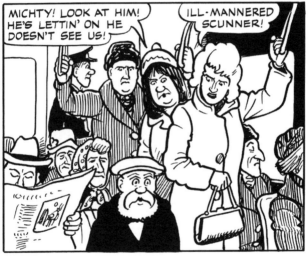

A gentleman will always offer a lady their seat.

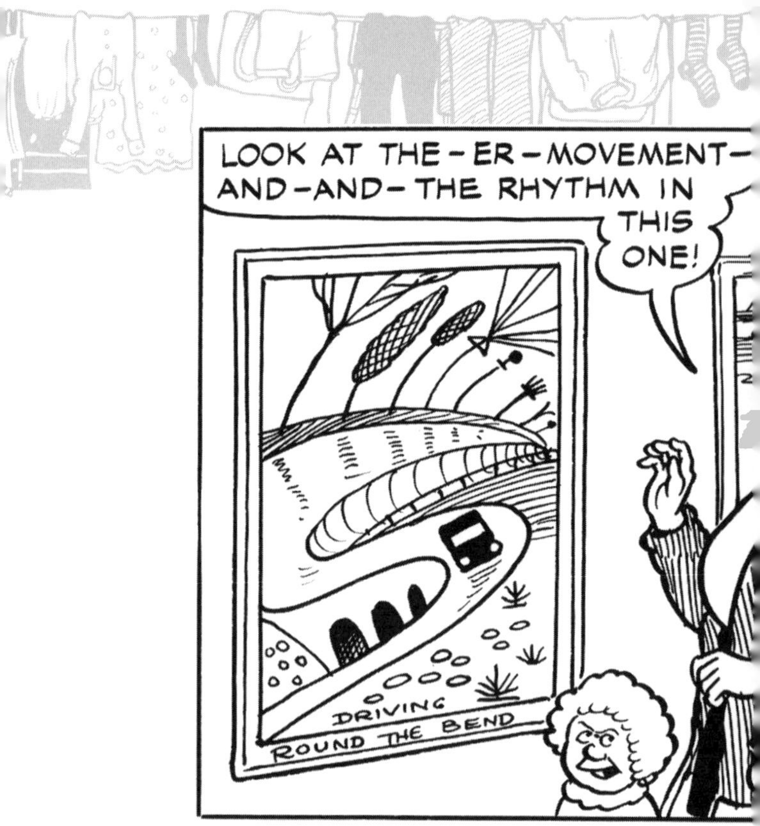
LOOK AT THE - ER - MOVEMENT - AND - AND - THE RHYTHM IN THIS ONE!
DRIVING ROUND THE BEND

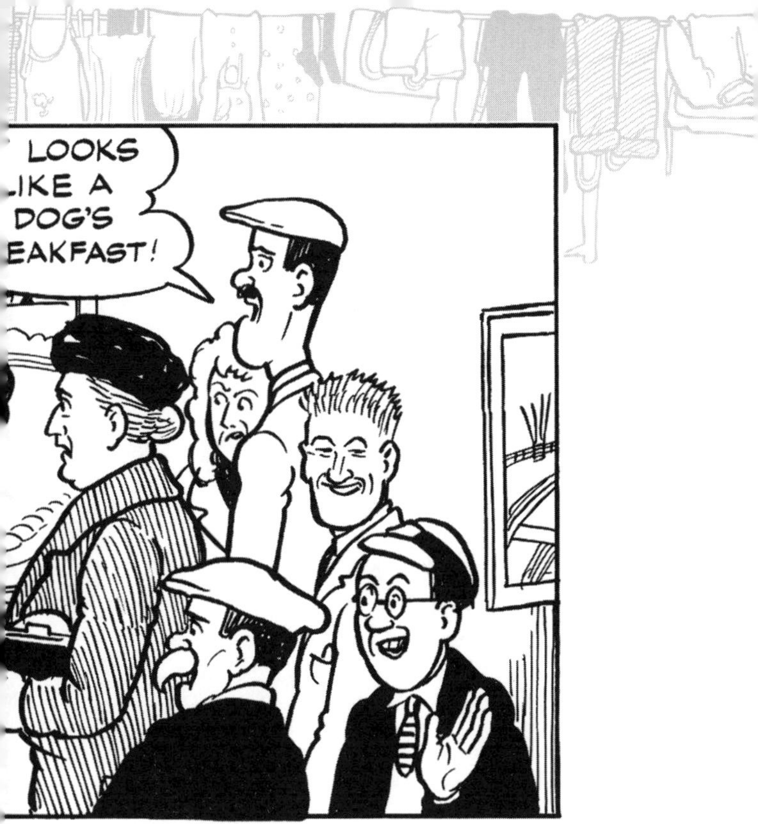
LOOKS
IKE A
DOG'S
EAKFAST!

Keep an open mind when
it comes to art and culture.

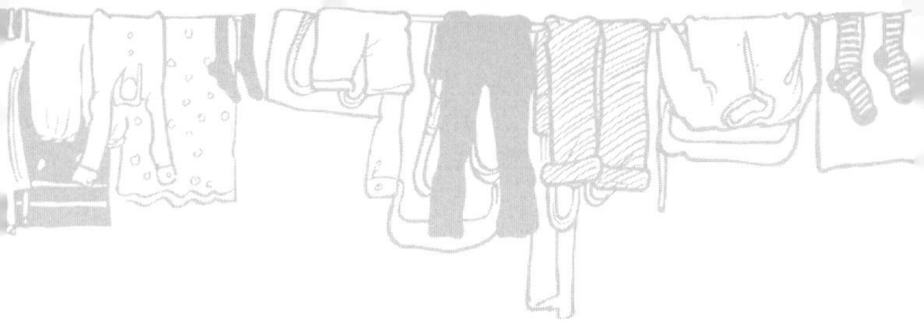

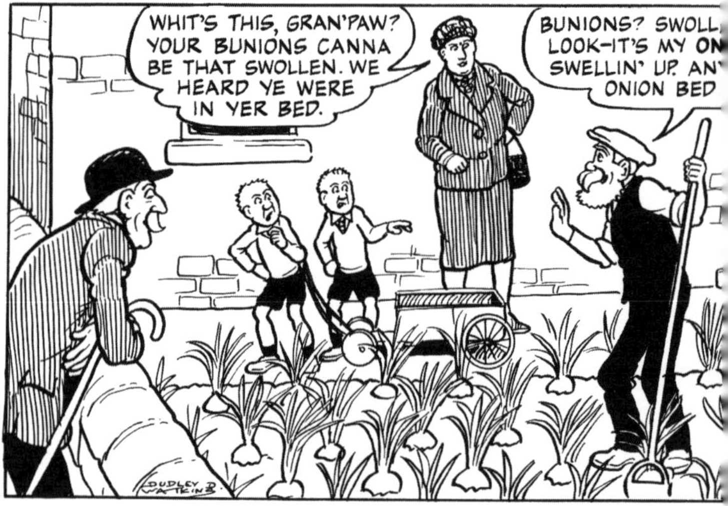
WHIT'S THIS, GRAN'PAW? YOUR BUNIONS CANNA BE THAT SWOLLEN. WE HEARD YE WERE IN YER BED.
BUNIONS? SWOLL LOOK—IT'S MY ON SWELLIN' UP. AN ONION BED
DUDLEY D. WATKINS

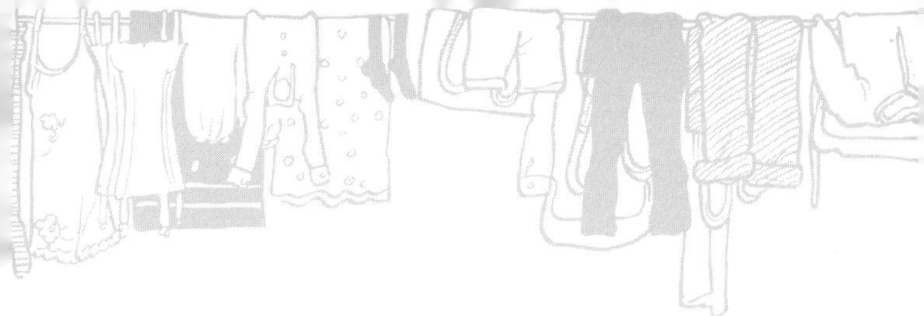

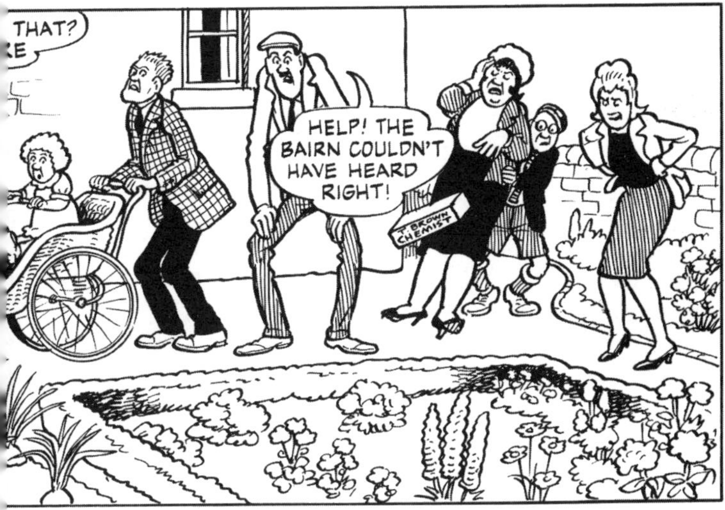
THAT?
HELP! THE BAIRN COULDN'T HAVE HEARD RIGHT!
T. BROWN CHEMIST

Be careful not to get
the wrong end of the stick.

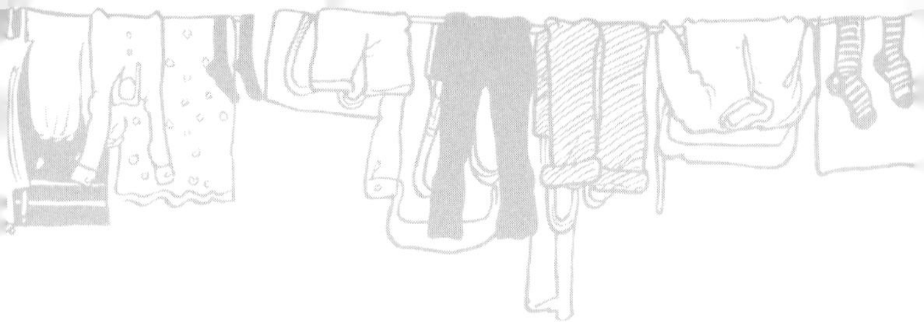

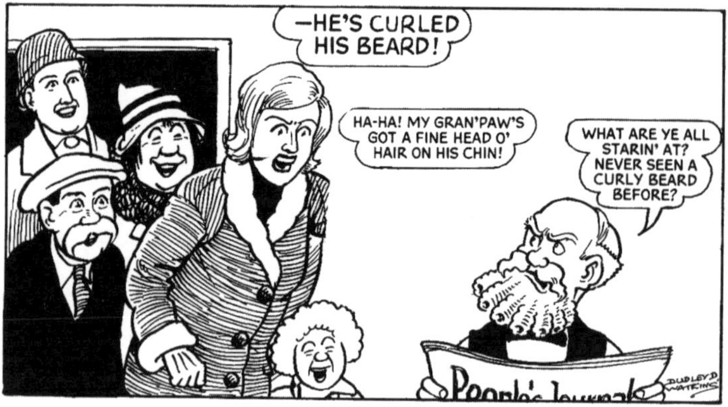

—HE'S CURLED HIS BEARD!
HA-HA! MY GRAN'PAW'S GOT A FINE HEAD O' HAIR ON HIS CHIN!
WHAT ARE YE ALL STARIN' AT? NEVER SEEN A CURLY BEARD BEFORE?
DUDLEY D WATKINS

Men should not be afraid to embrace beauty treatments.

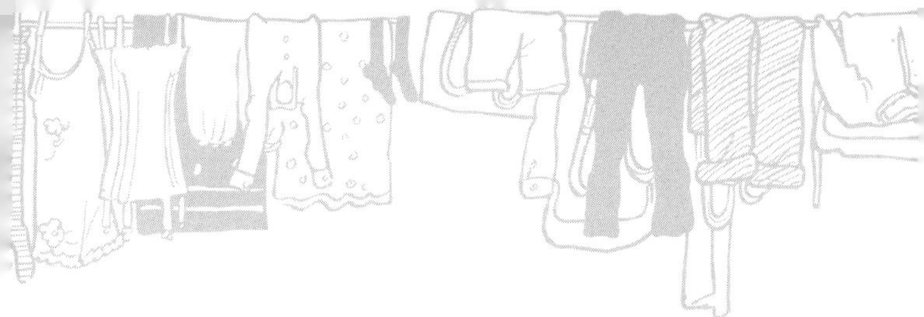

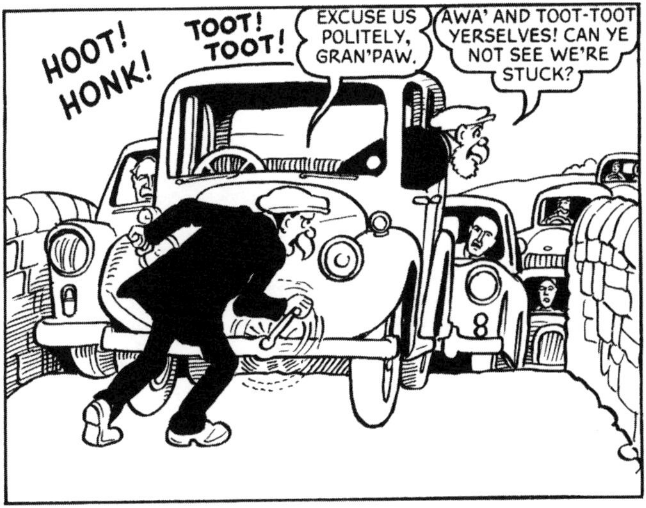
HOOT! HONK!
TOOT! TOOT!
EXCUSE US POLITELY, GRAN'PAW.
AWA' AND TOOT-TOOT YERSELVES! CAN YE NOT SEE WE'RE STUCK?

A friendly apology goes a long way.

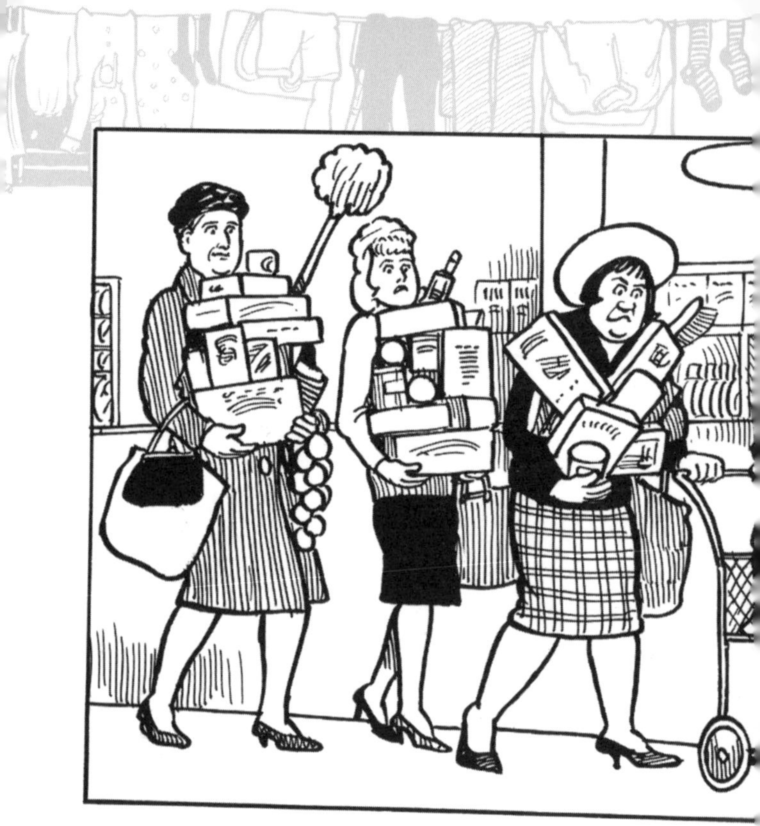

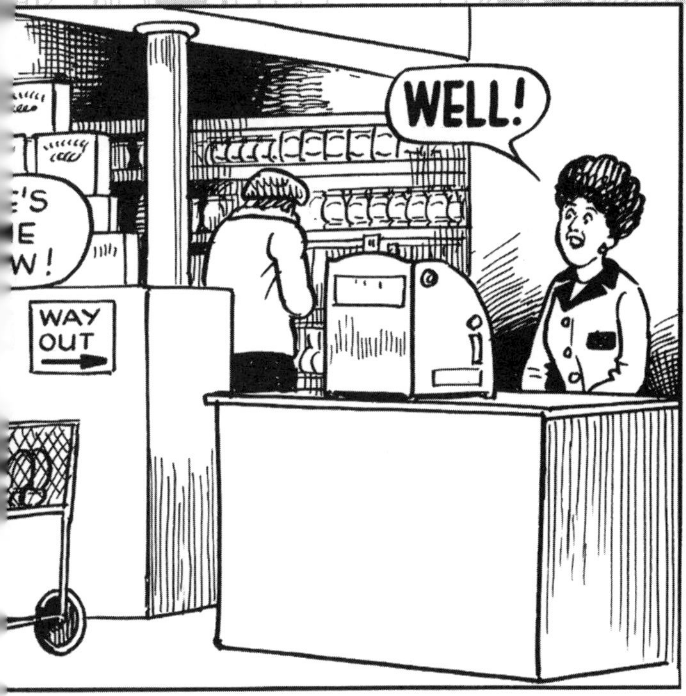
WELL!
WAY OUT

Do not let the weekly shop
stress you out.

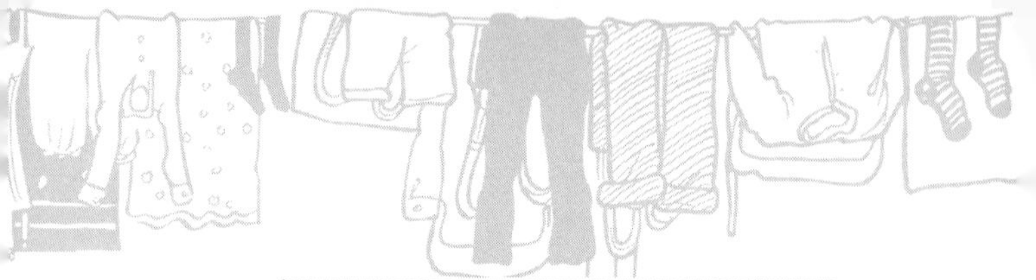

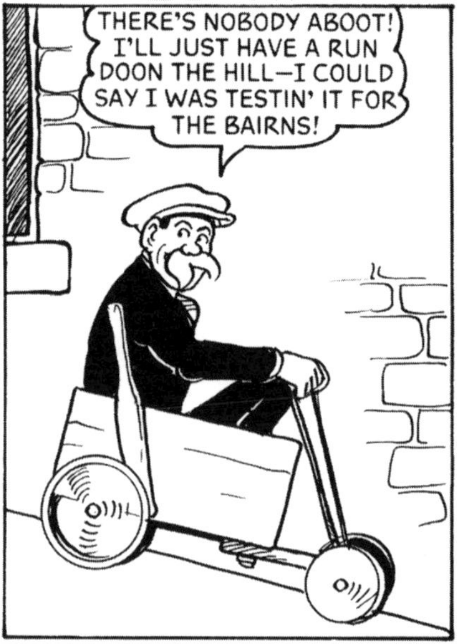
THERE'S NOBODY ABOOT! I'LL JUST HAVE A RUN DOON THE HILL—I COULD SAY I WAS TESTIN' IT FOR THE BAIRNS!

It is important to
stay young at heart.

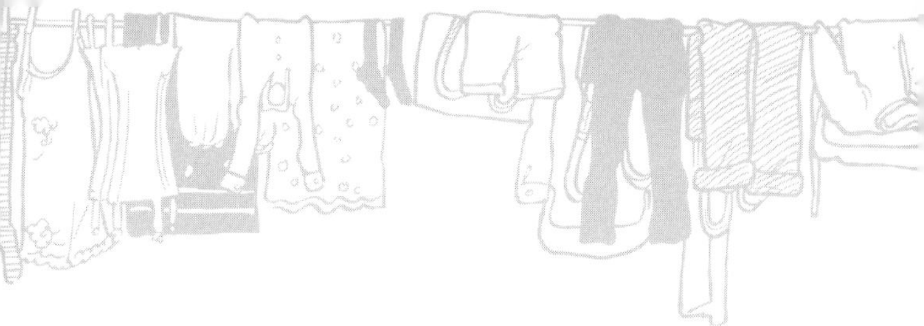

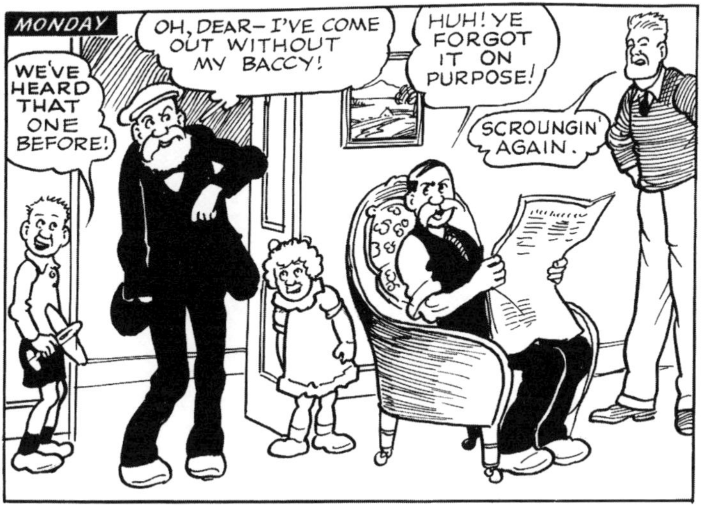
MONDAY
OH, DEAR—I'VE COME OUT WITHOUT MY BACCY!
WE'VE HEARD THAT ONE BEFORE!
HUH! YE FORGOT IT ON PURPOSE!
SCROUNGIN' AGAIN.

Be creative when it comes to cutting costs.

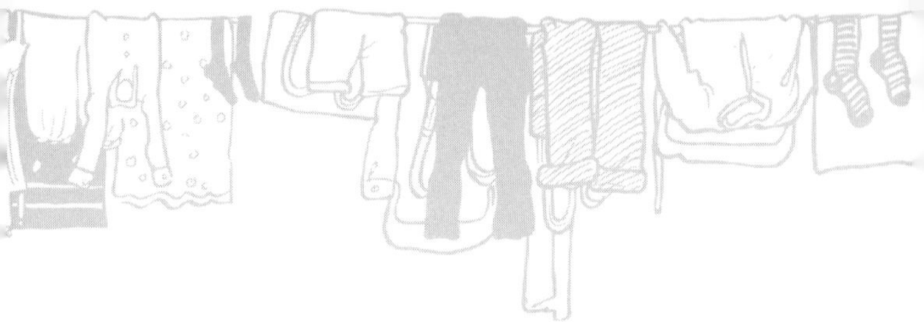

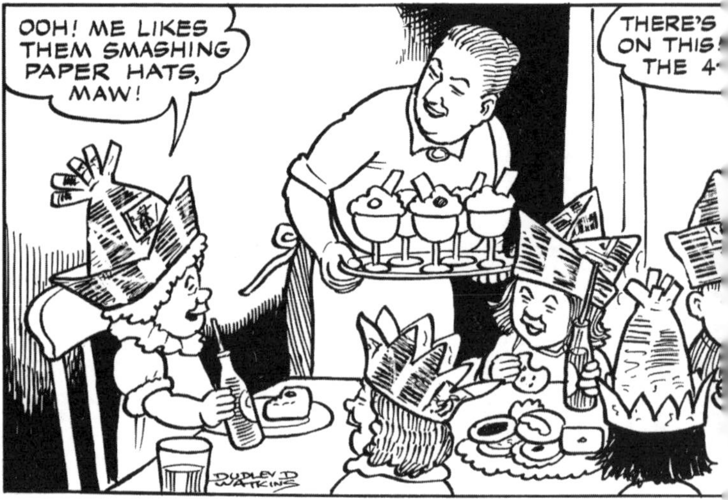

OOH! ME LIKES THEM SMASHING PAPER HATS, MAW!
THERE'S ON THIS THE 4
DUDLEY D WATKINS

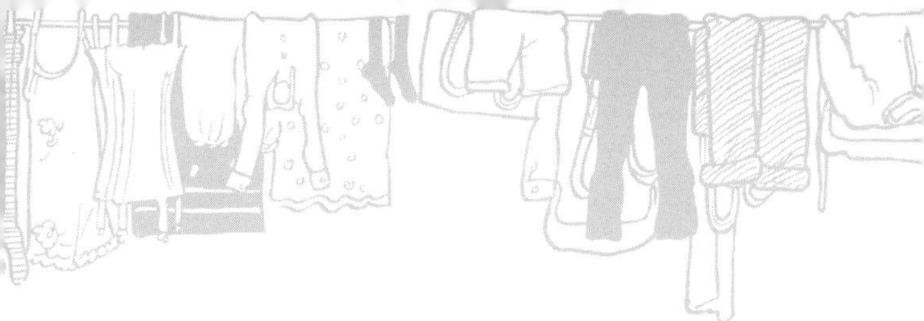

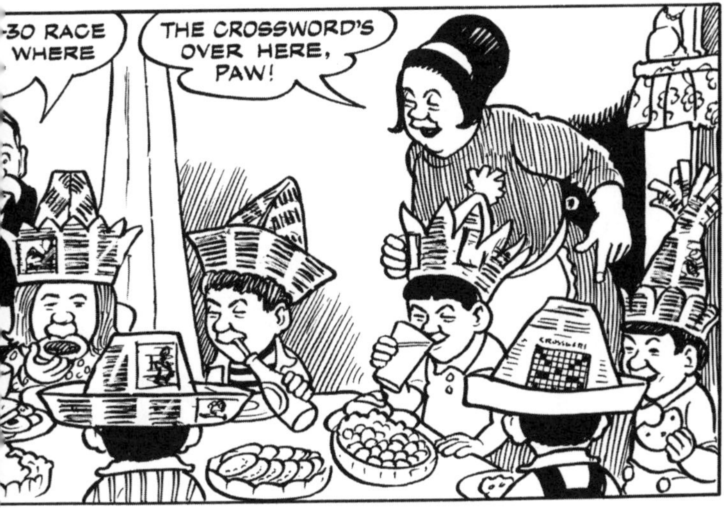
-30 RACE
WHERE
THE CROSSWORD'S
OVER HERE,
PAW!

Always remember to recycle
OLD newspapers.

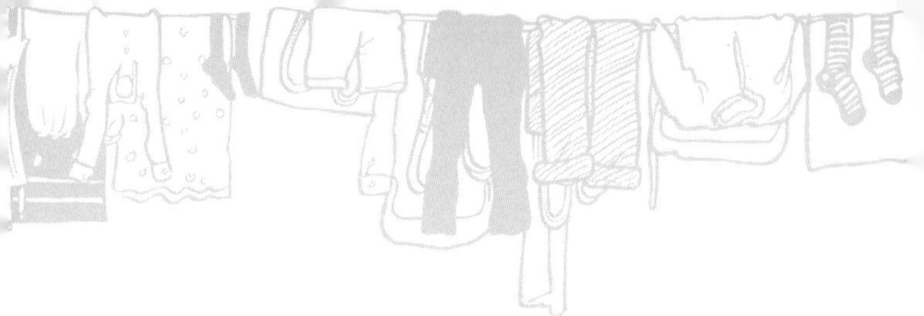

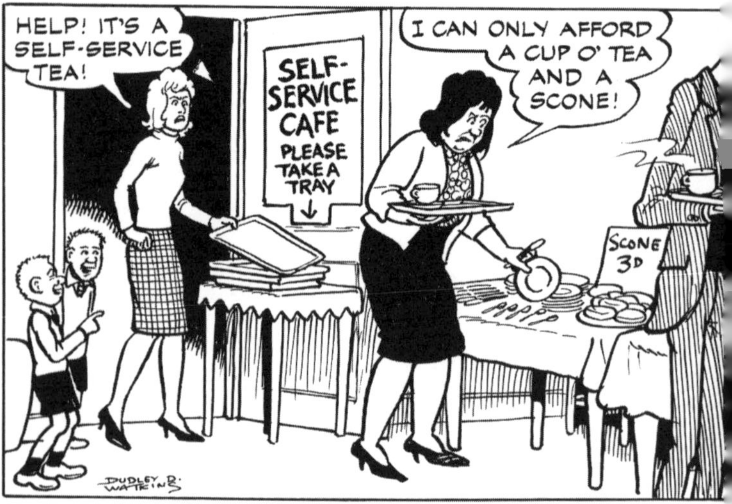
HELP! IT'S A SELF-SERVICE TEA!
SELF-SERVICE CAFE
PLEASE TAKE A TRAY
I CAN ONLY AFFORD A CUP O' TEA AND A SCONE!
SCONE 3D
DUDLEY D. WATKINS

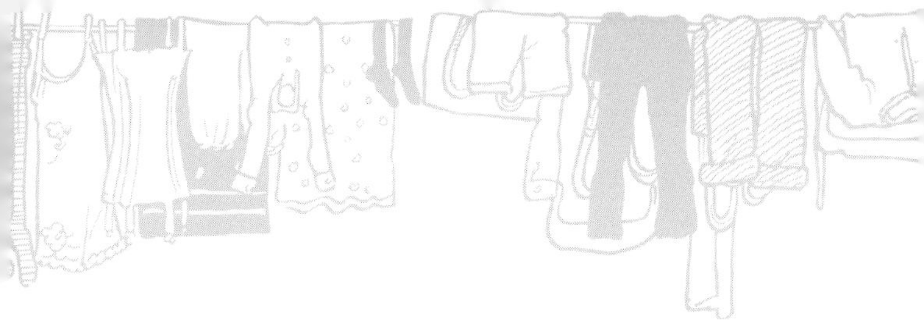

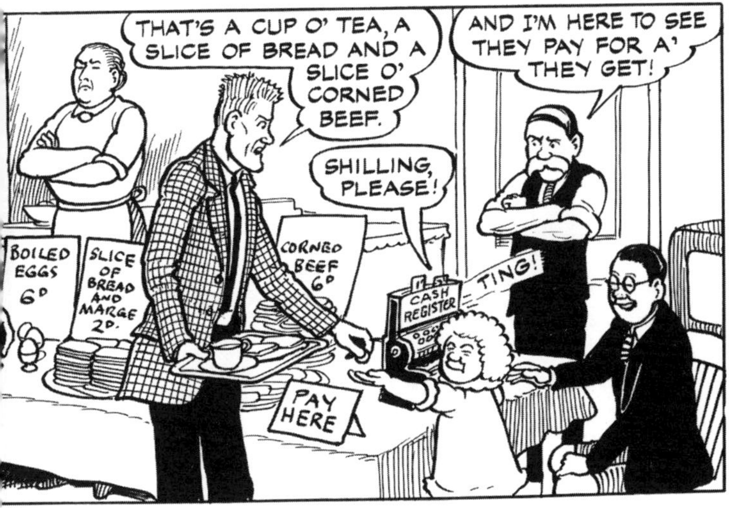
THAT'S A CUP O' TEA, A SLICE OF BREAD AND A SLICE O' CORNED BEEF.
SHILLING, PLEASE!
AND I'M HERE TO SEE THEY PAY FOR A' THEY GET!
BOILED EGGS 6D
SLICE OF BREAD AND MARGE 2D.
CORNED BEEF 6D
CASH REGISTER
TING!
PAY HERE

Do not take your parents' generosity for granted.

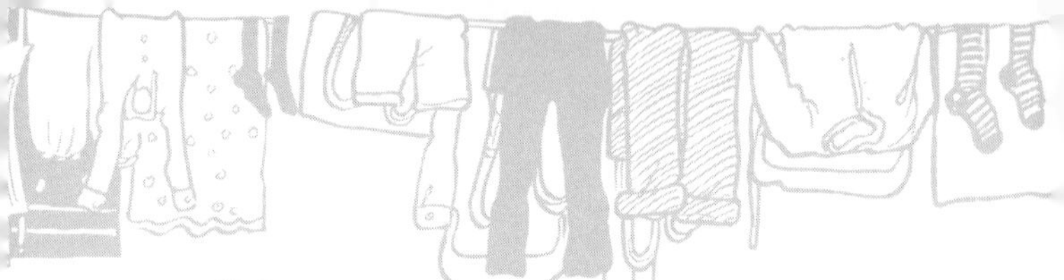

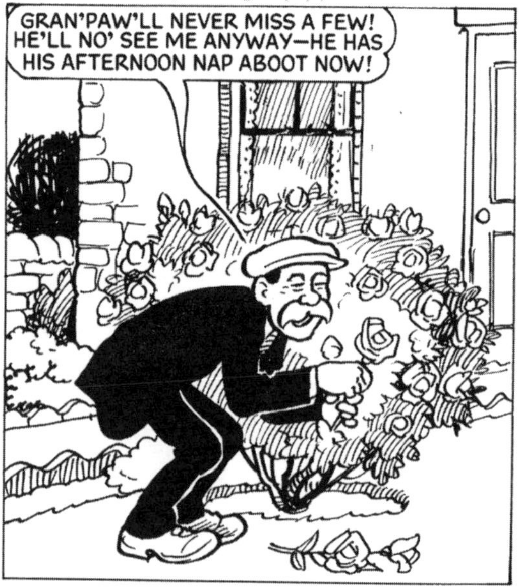
GRAN'PAW'LL NEVER MISS A FEW! HE'LL NO' SEE ME ANYWAY—HE HAS HIS AFTERNOON NAP ABOOT NOW!

Be as generous as you can when it comes to treating your wife.

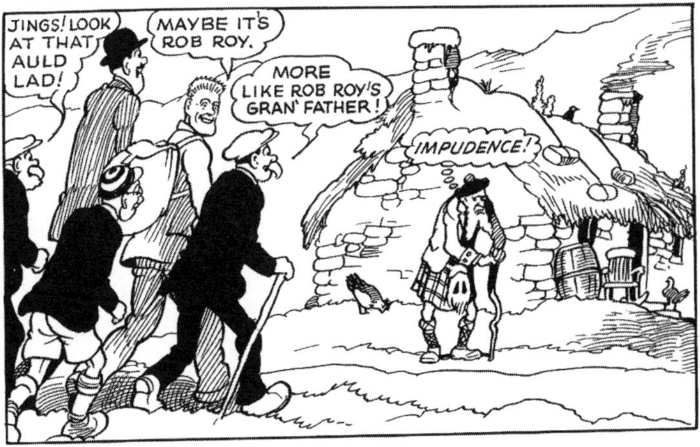
JINGS! LOOK AT THAT AULD LAD!
MAYBE IT'S ROB ROY.
MORE LIKE ROB ROY'S GRAN' FATHER!
IMPUDENCE!

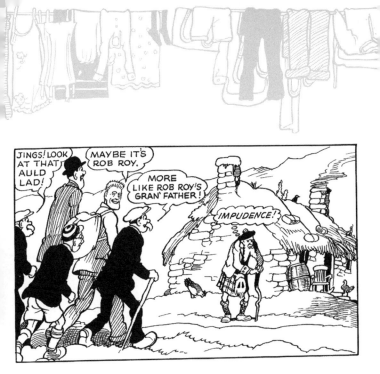

Respect your elders.

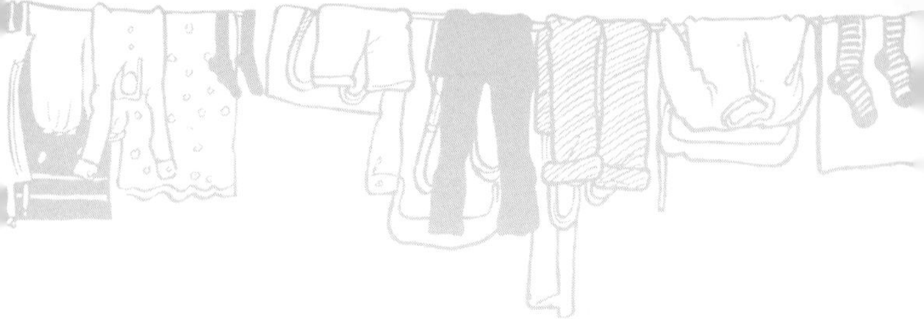

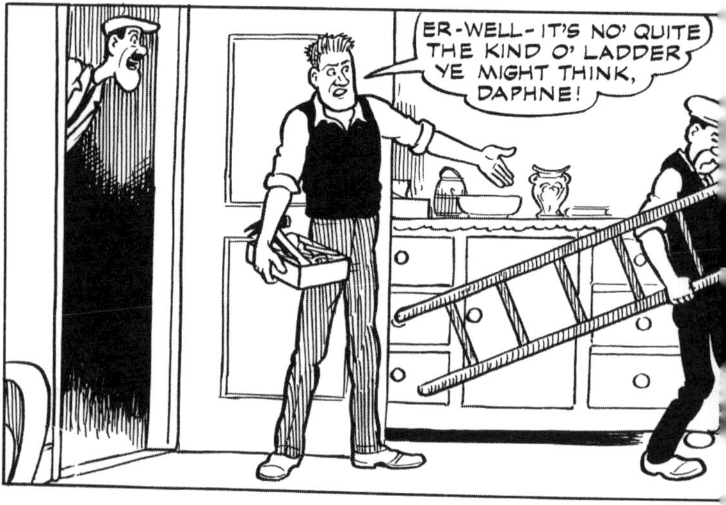
ER-WELL-IT'S NO' QUITE THE KIND O' LADDER YE MIGHT THINK, DAPHNE!

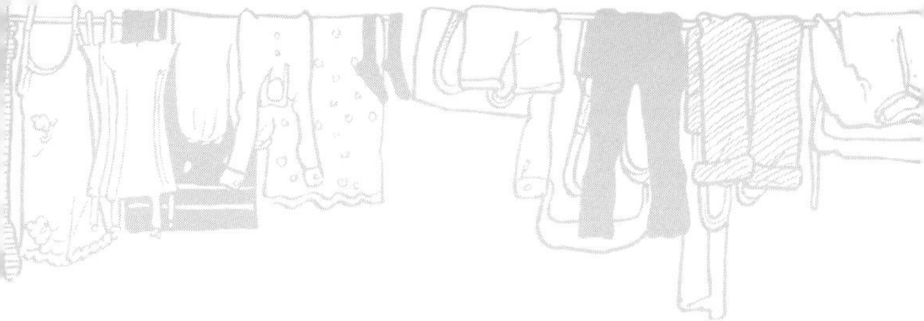

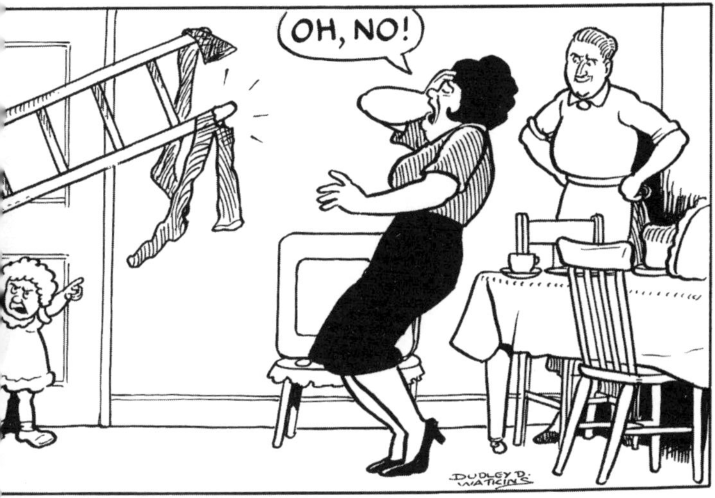
OH, NO!
DUDLEY D. WATKINS

Take care to avoid ladders
in your tights.

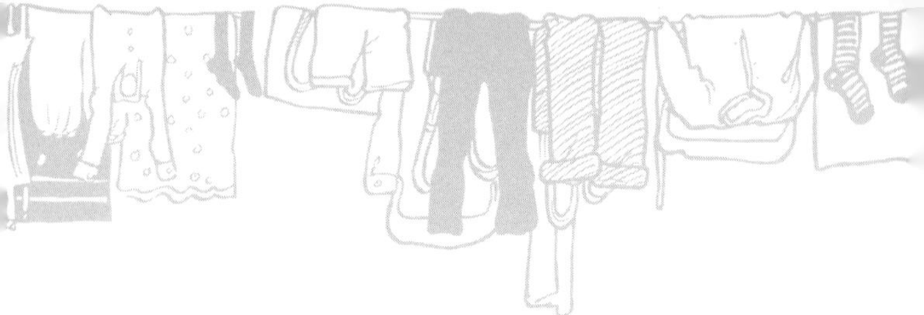

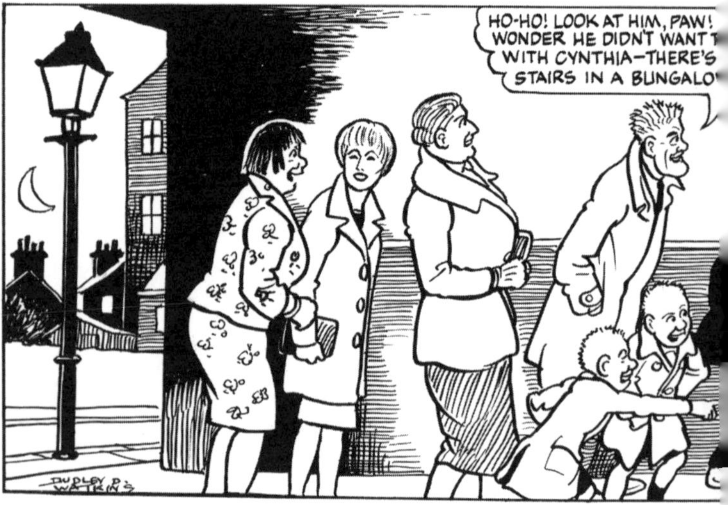
HO-HO! LOOK AT HIM, PAW! WONDER HE DIDN'T WANT T WITH CYNTHIA—THERE'S STAIRS IN A BUNGALO
DUDLEY D. WATKINS

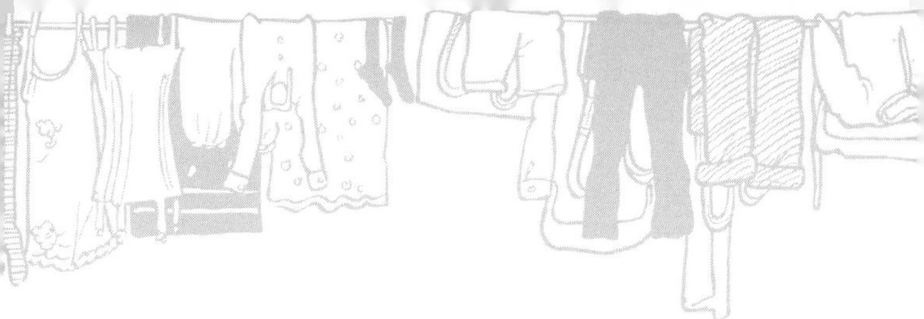

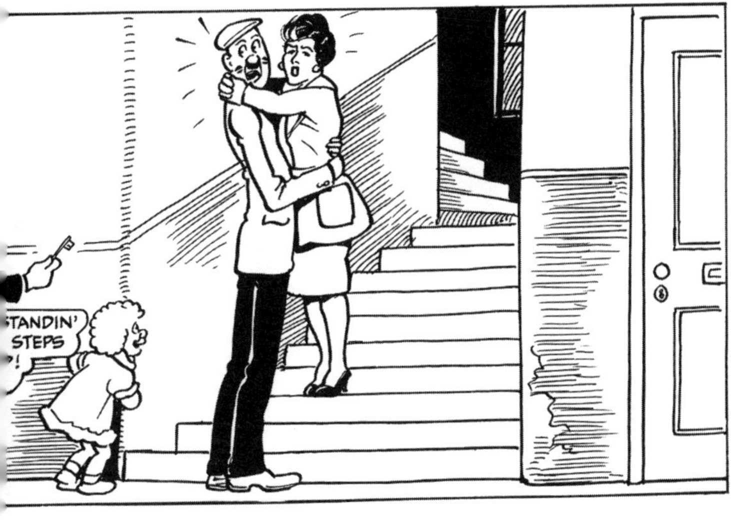
TANDIN'
STEPS
?!

Love can overcome
any obstacles.

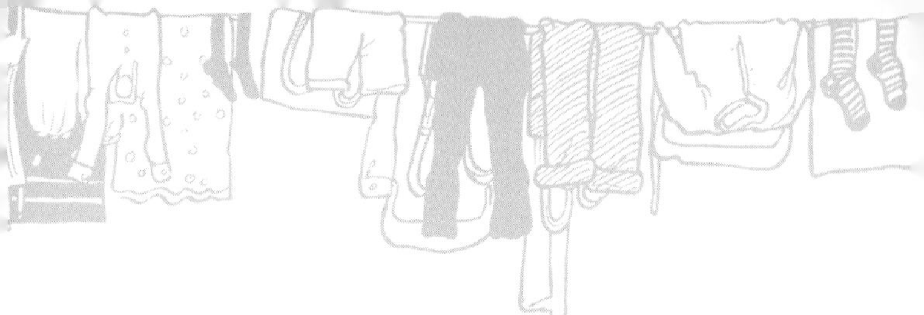

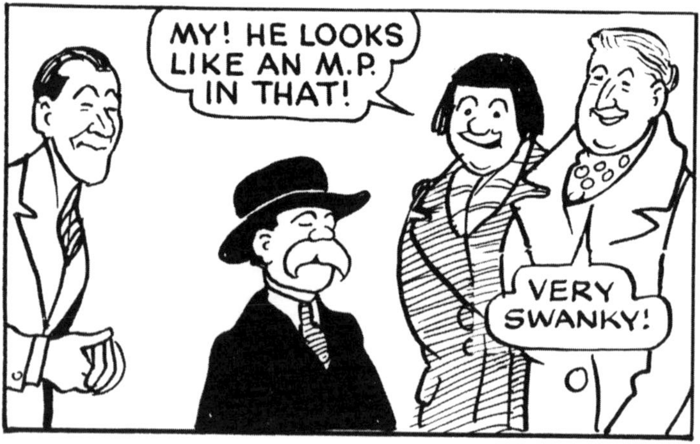
MY! HE LOOKS LIKE AN M.P. IN THAT!
VERY SWANKY!

A new accessory can go a long way in reinventing your wardrobe.

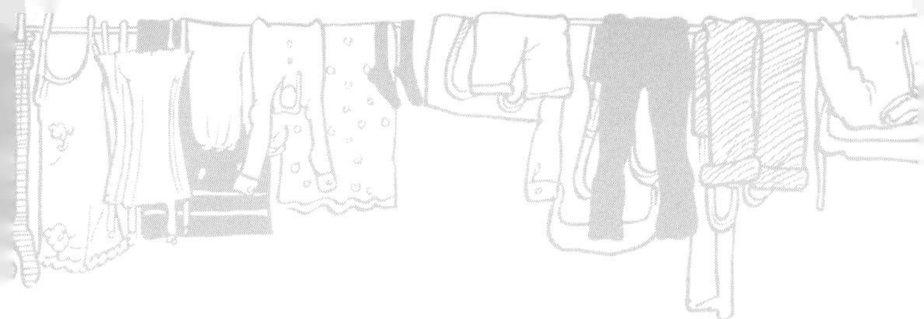

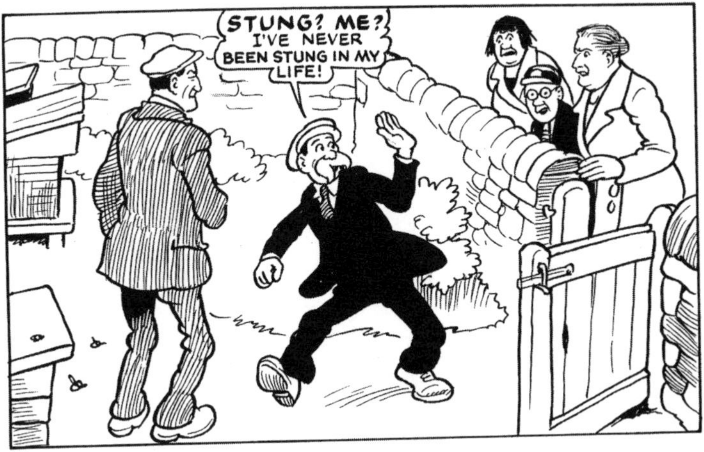
STUNG? ME? I'VE NEVER BEEN STUNG IN MY LIFE!

Try not to tempt fate.

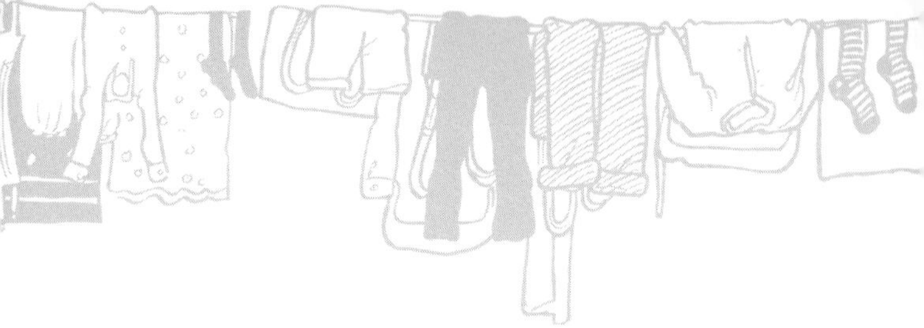

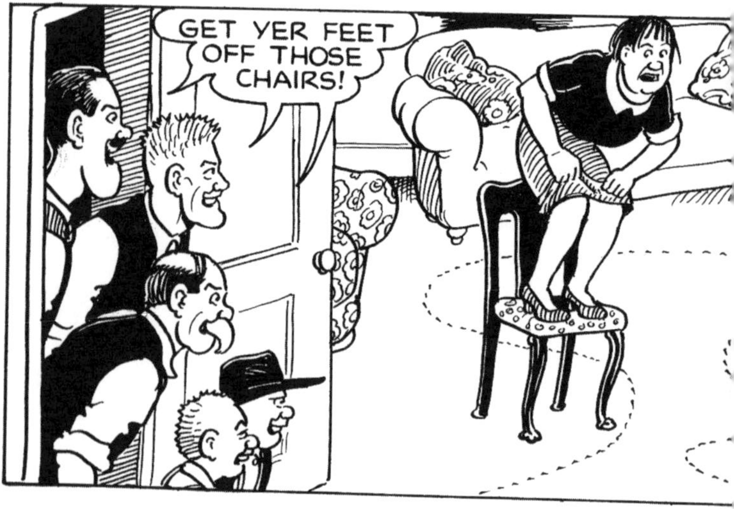
GET YER FEET OFF THOSE CHAIRS!

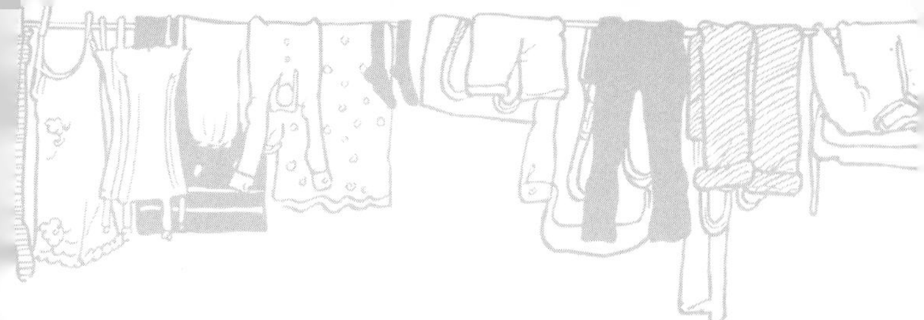

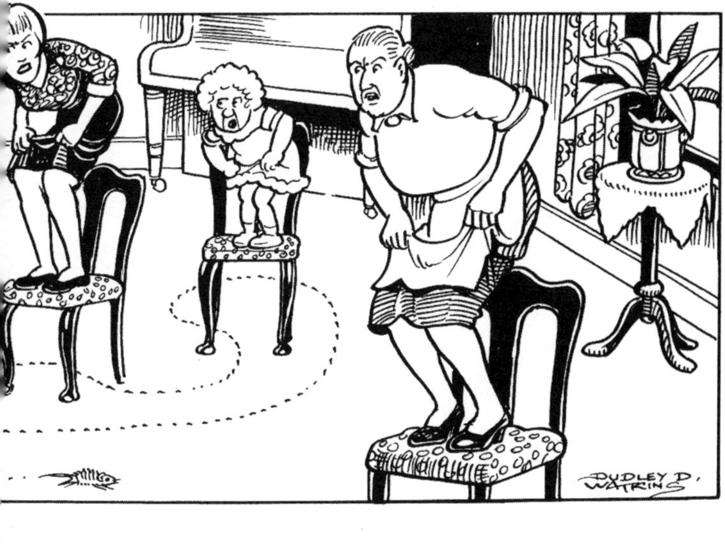
DUDLEY D. WATKINS

Always keep your feet
off the furniture.

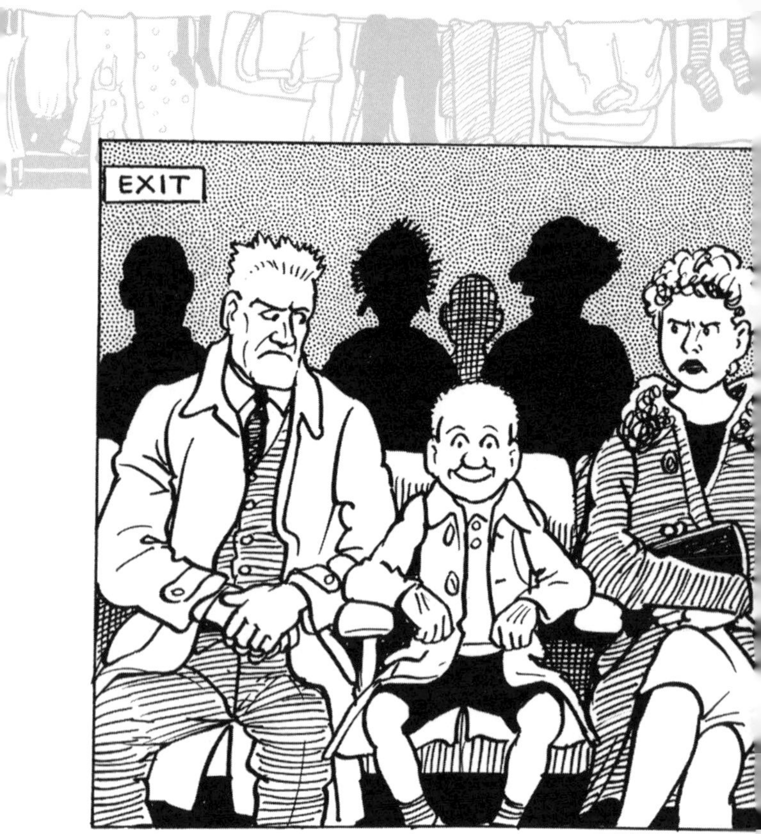
EXIT

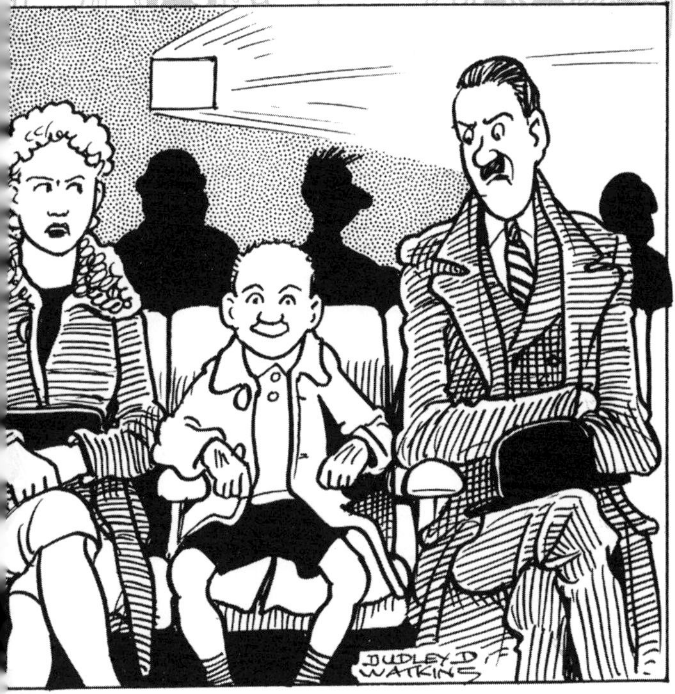
DUDLEY D WATKINS

t feels good to treat younger family members to a night at the pictures.

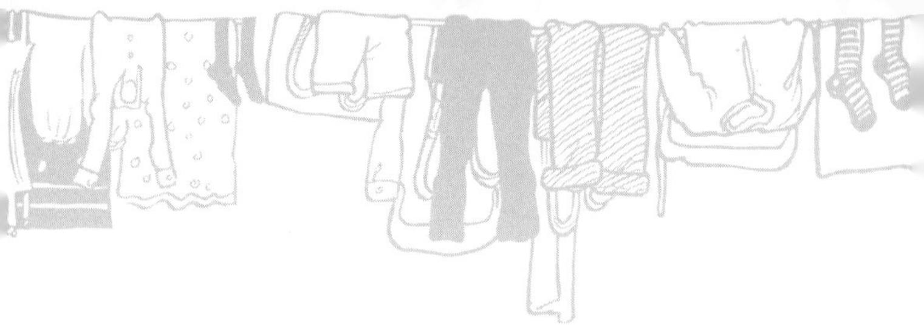

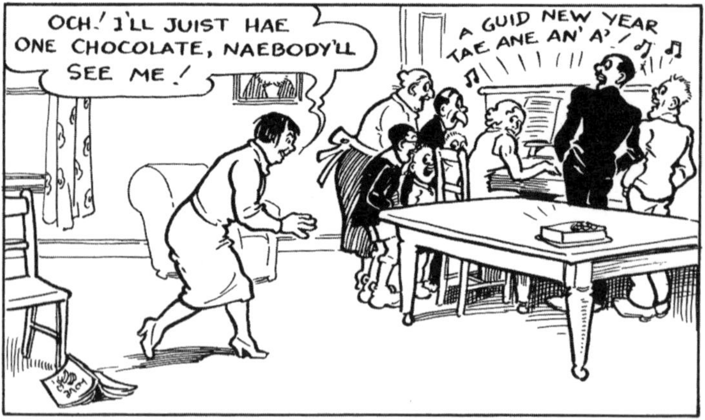
OCH! I'LL JUIST HAE ONE CHOCOLATE, NAEBODY'LL SEE ME!
A GUID NEW YEAR TAE ANE AN' A'!

Only make resolutions
that you can keep.

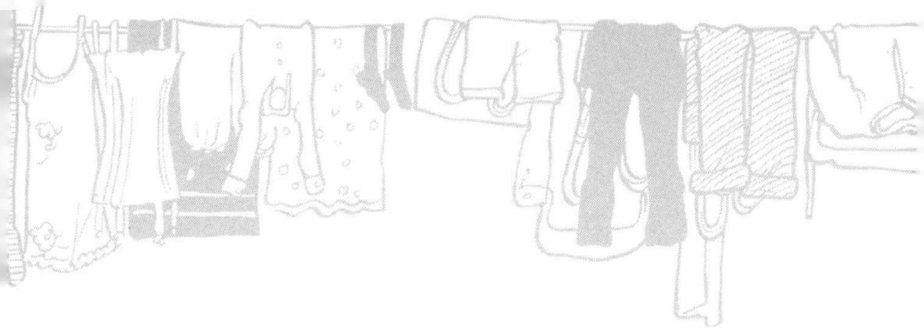

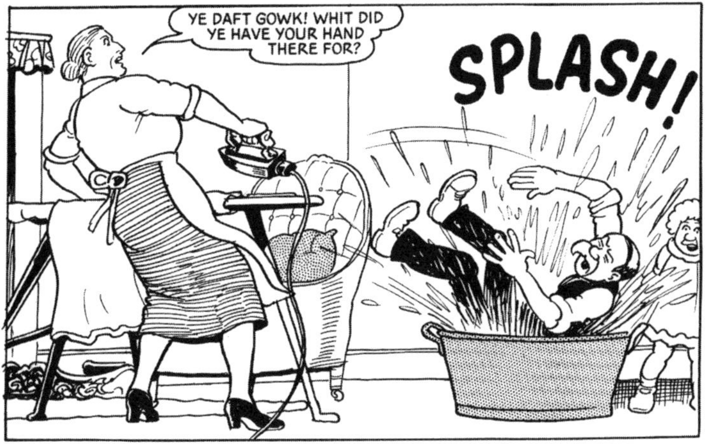
YE DAFT GOWK! WHIT DID YE HAVE YOUR HAND THERE FOR?
SPLASH!

Safety First!

FATHER'S DAY'S OVER–
SO YOU CAN CHASE YERSELF!
SEE!

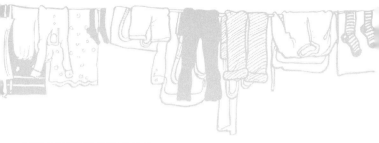

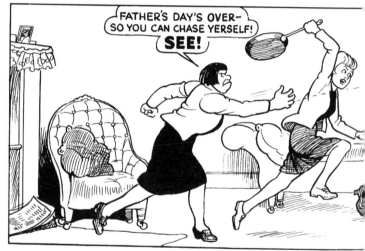

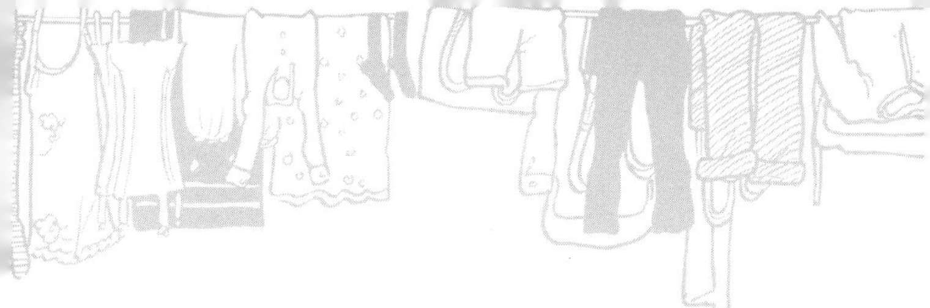

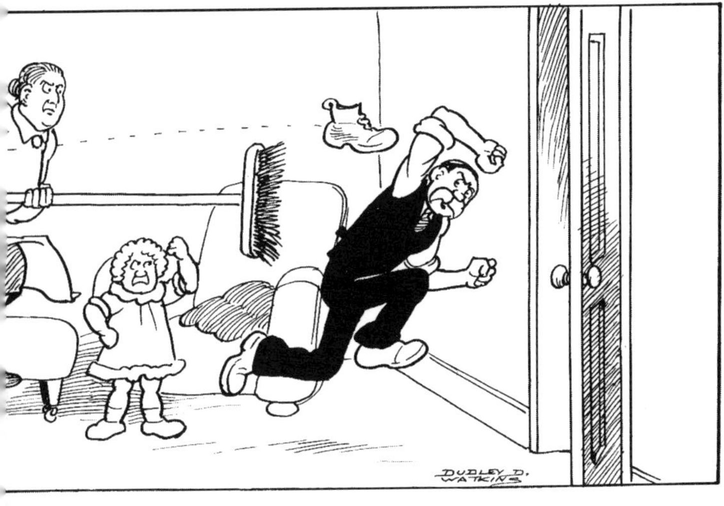
DUDLEY D.
WATKINS

Father's Day is the perfect time to celebrate the man of the house.

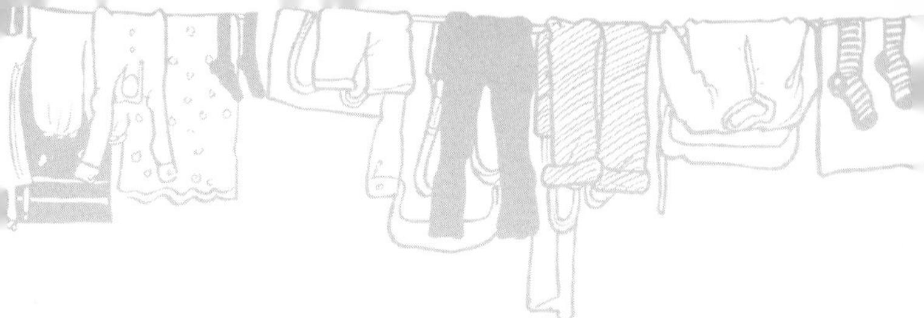

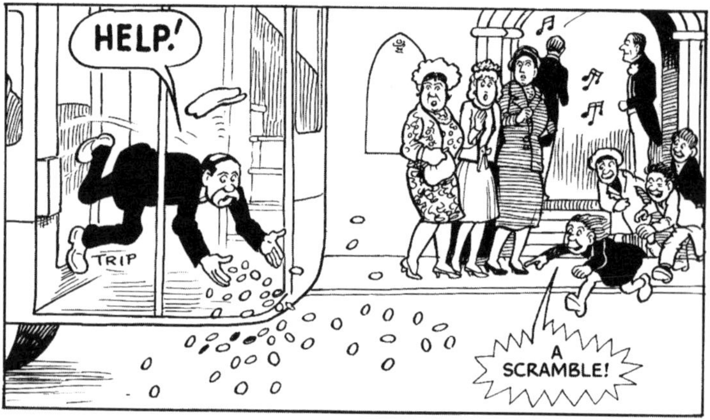
HELP!
TRIP
A SCRAMBLE!

Be generous to children.

HOW ABOUT THIS ONE, PAW? MAKE'S MAW LOOK YEARS YOUNGER!
NEVER! IT'S JUST A MESS!

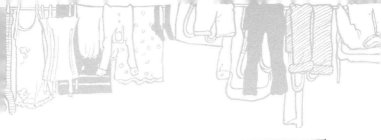

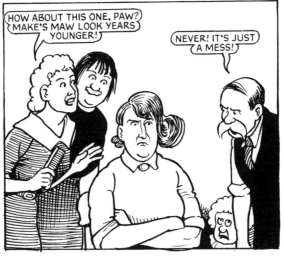

Don't be afraid to change with the times.

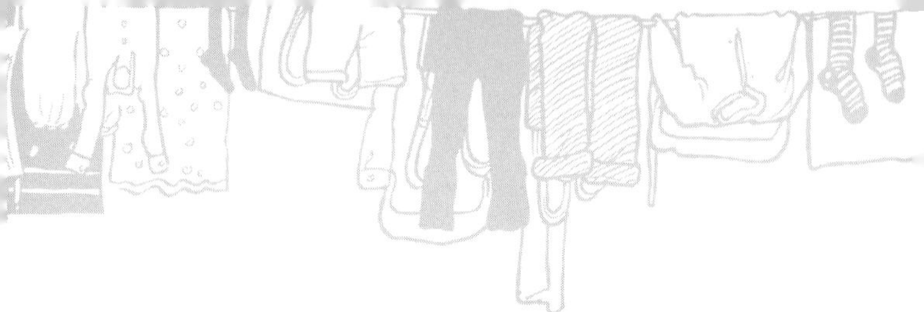

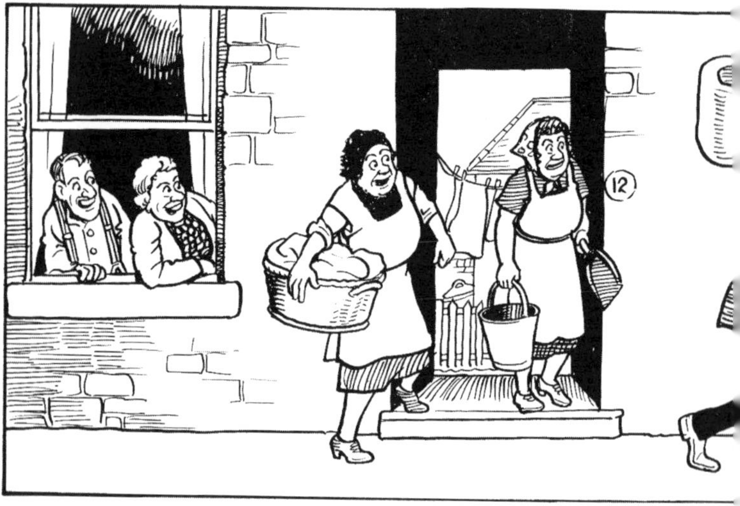
12

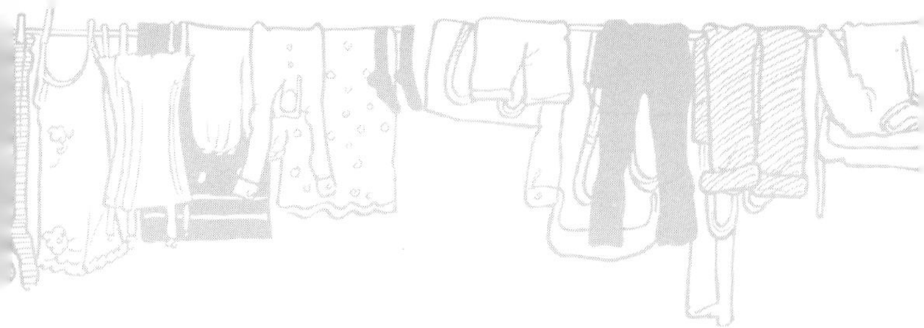

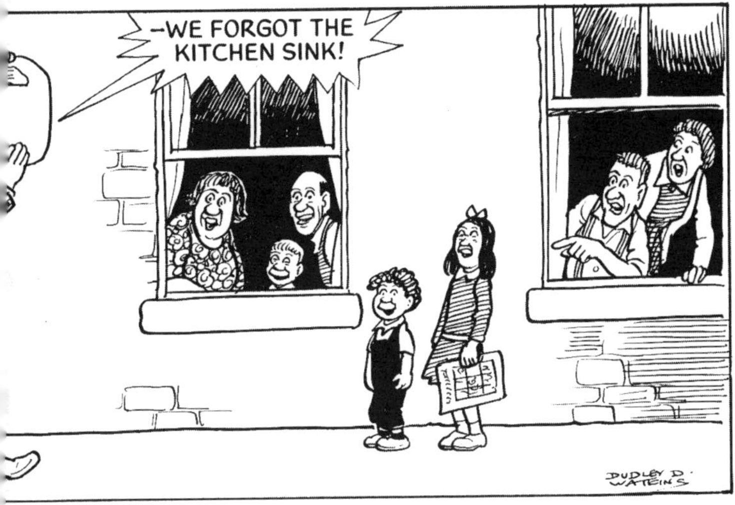
–WE FORGOT THE KITCHEN SINK!
DUDLEY D. WATKINS

Make sure to pack everything when going on holiday.

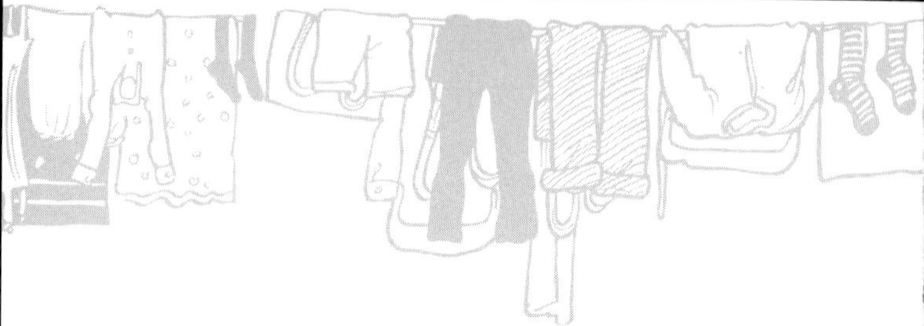

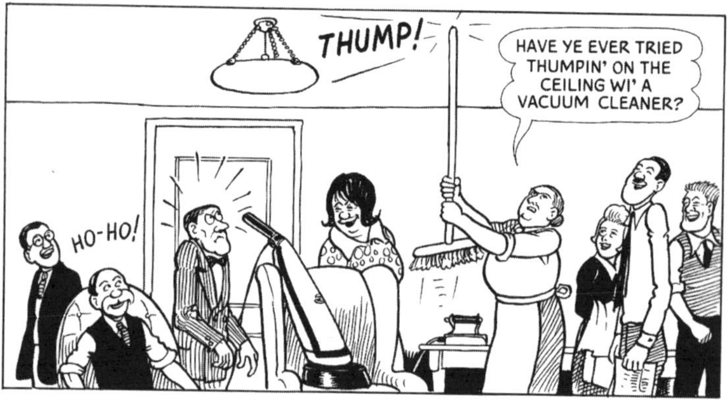
THUMP!
HAVE YE EVER TRIED THUMPIN' ON THE CEILING WI' A VACUUM CLEANER?
HO-HO!

Old-fashioned beats
new-fangled any day!